An Administrator's Handbook On Designing Programs for the GIFTED AND TALENTED

June B. Jordan and John A. Grossi
Editors

A product of the ERIC Clearinghouse on Handicapped and Gifted Children.

Published in 1980 jointly by The Council for Exceptional Children and its Division, the Association for the Gifted (TAG), 1920 Association Drive, Reston, Virginia 22091.

Second Printing 1984

Library of Congress Card Catalog Number 80-68984

ISBN 0-86586-112-9

This publication was prepared with funding from the National Institute of Education, US Department of Education, under contract no. 400-76-0119. Contractors undertaking such projects under government sponsorship are encouraged to express freely their judgment in professional and technical matters. Prior to publication the manuscript was submitted to The Council for Exceptional Children for critical review and determination of professional competence. This publication has met such standards. Points of view, however, do not necessarily represent the official view or opinions of either The Council for Exceptional Children, the National Institute of Education, or the Department of Education.

Printed in the United States of America.

Contents

List of Figures, Forms, and Tables

About the Authors

Mary Mack Frasier, Ph.D., is Associate Professor of Educational Psychology and Coordinator, Program for the Gifted, at the University of Georgia, Athens. Dr. Frasier has worked with high potential culturally diverse youth at the middle school, high school, and college levels for 14 years and with graduate degree programs in gifted education for 6 years. She has done extensive consulting with school systems and universities at the local, state, national, and international levels, as well as with state departments of education, Educational Testing Service, and The National Center for Research in Vocational Education. Primarily, her research, publications, and consultations have been concerned with identification of and programing for culturally diverse gifted children. Other areas of research, publications, and consultations include public relations for teachers of the gifted and bibliotherapy for gifted and talented children.

John A. Grossi is Director of the Gifted and Talented Policy Information Project with The Council for Exceptional Children in Reston, Virginia. Mr. Grossi has been a teacher of the gifted and administrator of gifted programs in Florida and North Carolina. He has coordinated programs for handicapped children in Head Start at Florida State University and for gifted handicapped preschoolers in Chapel Hill, North Carolina. Mr. Grossi has consulted with federal, state, and local education agencies, and was an instructor in the Division of Creative Teaching at St. Leo College, Florida. He has authored publications addressing state and local policy effecting the education of the gifted, programing for the gifted handicapped, and parental involvement. He has also served as both a consultant and Task Force Advisory Committee member for the Office of Gifted and Talented in the US Department of Education.

Marie S. Gustin is Superintendent of Schools, New Britain, Connecticut, having previously served as Assistant Superintendent for Instruction, Guidance and Testing, and Special Services. Dr. Gustin's efforts as superintendent have focused on curriculum revision and an alliance between the school system and business and industry to strengthen career and vocational education programs. Past experience includes classroom teaching, undergraduate and graduate level teaching in psychology and educational psychology, as well as work as a psychologist at Children's Hospital Medical Center of Harvard University. She serves on the advisory board of the International Federation of Learning Disabilities.

Edwina D. Pendarvis coordinates and teaches in the gifted education master's degree and certification programs at Marshall University, Huntington, West Virginia. She directs Marshall's summer enrichment program for gifted children, and serves as liaison with a local school district in an experimental program offering college courses to gifted junior high and high school students. Dr. Pendarvis has experience as a classroom teacher and served as a resource room teacher in the gifted program in Pasco County, Florida. More recently, she worked with the Kentucky Department of Education as director of a federally funded grant to develop and provide inservice training in the education of exceptional children.

Joyce Van Tassel is currently director of a regional gifted center that provides program development assistance to over 95 school districts in Illinois. She was formerly director of the Illinois Gifted Program, coordinator of gifted programs in Toledo, Ohio, and a teacher of gifted high school students in English and Latin. She has worked as a consultant on gifted education in over 25 states and for key national groups, including the US Department of Education, Leadership Training Institute, National Association of Independent Schools, and American Association of School Administrators. She currently serves on editorial boards for *The Journal for the Education of the Gifted* and *Roeper Review*, and is past president of CEC-TAG. She has taught courses in gifted education at seven major universities and written numerous articles in the field.

William G. Vassar is State Director of Programs for the Gifted and Talented for the Connecticut State Department of Education. He has worked with gifted and talented children and youth for the past 25 years as a teacher, secondary school principal, state director, visiting professor, and teacher trainer. He has served as President of The Association for the Gifted (TAG), the National Association for Gifted Children (NAGC), and the Council of State Directors of Programs for the Gifted (CSDPG). He has served as a Coordinator of President Johnson's White House Task Force on the Gifted and Talented, and was a consultant and staff member of the Marland Report on the Gifted and Talented to the US Congress. In addition, he has served as a professional consultant to both the Senate and House Subcommittees on Education relating to the gifted and talented. Throughout the years, he has published and lectured widely on the gifted and talented.

CHAPTER 1

Special Educational Programs for the Gifted Are Essential—A Superintendent's Point of View

MARIE S. GUSTIN

Everyone is talking about the energy crisis today. A professional friend of mine told me that when energy changes from one form to another the total amount remains the same. I do not know physics, but I do know the young people in this country. They are our greatest source of energy. They are the powerhouse that will keep this nation going. With the unlimited energy of their minds, bodies, and spirit they can turn this energy crisis into a challenge. Because of them, I know the future is in good hands. Luckily, they are inheriting a country that still has the ability to give them the right to their own individuality, which we as educators cherish and protect with passion and hope.

THE BROAD MISSION OF EDUCATION

Although schools are constantly involved with a variety of issues and tasks, the process and quality of student learning continues to be a most important concern. Schools are expected to be strong and stable; to be committed to the highest ideals; to teach all the basics and a great deal more to learners of all ages, cultures, and languages; to attempt to correct all the social ills—and to do it all at a modest cost and with limited human resources. Schools have performed that miracle because, in spite of staggering problems, they continue to grow in positive ways.

In many areas, educators are moving forward and breaking important new ground, forming alliances which will make education more meaningful for the children we serve. Our strategy has been to build on the strengths of the existing system, reflect the forces of change in society, and serve as agents of constructive change. No other investment that we as adults can make for our children will exceed education in yielding economic and social dividends.

As educators it is our responsibility and privilege to provide for all children who come to us, preparing them to take their rightful place in life: the advantaged as well as the disadvantaged, the gifted and talented as well as the mentally and physically handicapped, the college bound as well as the vocationally oriented, and the multitude of children who make up the mainstream of the student body. The mission is clear: our primary concern is to guide our children toward becoming self sufficient, mature, and contributory citizens with a sense of genuine values and positive attitudes who meet the demands of life with skills, knowledge, confidence, and productivity.

The ongoing challenge for educators is to deal with the many and varied spiraling issues and needs of the day whose solutions require meticulous and responsible planning and quality implementation. Positive achievements require participation and cooperation from staff representing a variety of interests and expertise and a community that has aspirations for and commitment toward its youth.

MEETING THE NEEDS OF THE GIFTED AND TALENTED

Numbers of students in our schools possess extraordinary learning abilities and specialized talents to such a degree that their needs cannot completely be met in a regular school program. Special educational programs for the gifted and talented are a logical and essential part of any school program which recognizes and respects individual differences among its pupils.

The philosophy which guides this special application is based on the belief (1) that each child is a unique human being who possesses individual educational needs and abilities; and (2) that it is the responsibility of our schools first to identify those needs and abilities and then to provide the kinds of educational experiences that hold the greatest potential for meeting individual needs and developing each child's abilities to the fullest degree.

Educators have shown interest in the gifted child for many years. Only recently, however, has the American public shown a growing understanding and a deeper awareness of the problem of educating the gifted child. The reasons for the surge of public interest in what the schools are doing for the gifted are several, including the recognition of the unique value of the individual and the reality of social need. Reasons for past neglect in providing an adequate education for the gifted include indifference, fear, hostility, misgivings, and lack of knowledge. The feeling prevailed too, that individual attention to the gifted would mean less attention to other children, resulting in an undemocratic situation. It was assumed that a talented child would get by without special help. The trend now, fortunately, is to develop the resources of these children for a twofold purpose: for the good of the child and for the good of humanity.

An effective program for the gifted does what education should do for all types of individuals. It makes the most of each child's ability and helps him or her to live more fully in the present as well as to prepare for the future. The basic goal differs only in its greater emphasis on creative ability and effort, initiative, critical thinking, social adjustment, responsibility, and the development of unselfish qualities of leadership. Although these objectives are desirable for all students, they are essential for the gifted.

NURTURING INDIVIDUAL DIFFERENCES

The diversity among children is sometimes exceedingly great. The range of ways in which children must be treated is equally great. All educators are in agreement that meeting the special educational needs of the intellectually gifted requires intensive and individualized planning. How can gifted children develop and use their potential? Through what means can this be accomplished? Answers to these questions merit attention and have been topics of debate for many years. Yet a variety of problems have fostered delay in making provisions for the gifted, and, as a result, these students have been neglected.

Different types of procedures now in use for educating the gifted include the special school, special fulltime classes in the regular school, special groups (parttime classes), nursery school programs, enrichment provided in regular classrooms, special guidance and tutoring programs, and acceleration. In all of these, enrichment predominates. No single plan of educating gifted children is suitable for every situation and every child. Careful appraisal should be made of programs and results thus far attained. The findings are vital for further development and improvement in educational programing for the gifted.

The exceptional learning needs of the gifted child exist throughout life. One bulletin of special programs for gifted pupils, for example, stated that programs should be developed so that the exceptional needs of each child are continuously met as he or she progresses through school. A program which meets individual needs at one grade level and not at another is not a valid one.

Gifted children are not a homogenous group. The underachieving gifted child and the gifted child with a handicap represent two types of deviating gifted children who require special attention over and above the provisions made for gifted children in general.

Some children with high intellectual ability do not achieve. Some are actually failures in school. This fact indicates that it takes more than intelligence to succeed in school as well as in life. A study made on underachieving gifted children showed that the gifted underachiever is a kind of intellectual delinquent who withdraws from goals, activities, and active social participation in general. Initial attempts at creative accomplishment may not have been seen by others as worthwhile, but only as "queer" or "different." It is believed that blocking rewards for deviant achievement has blunted work drives and stifled creativity. Cultural differences in values and poor parental relationships may also contribute to the failure to achieve.

The man on the street expects the teacher to spot gifted children and do something for them, but various studies have shown that teachers do not do a very good job of recognizing the gifted child; in fact, they fail to identify 10% to 50% of the gifted. If given guidance in making observations, however, teachers can provide much significant information. In fact, their observations probably supply the greatest single resource (other than objective tests) in identifying gifted children.

Each gifted child is unique, and as a group gifted children cannot be organized under a single plan of education. Efforts to properly educate these children by one specific plan, such as acceleration, special classes, or enrichment in the regular grades are found to be inadequate in some situations.

EFFECTIVE PROGRAM PLANNING

Decisions on where to place a gifted child, how to organize for his or her education, and what teaching techniques and materials to use depend largely on the pattern of development of that particular child and the provisions for all children in the school system. Thus, a gifted child must be evaluated in terms of abilities, disabilities, interests, habits, home environment, and community values. The educational program can be better determined on the basis of this evaluation than by first setting up an educational program and then fitting all gifted children into it. Whatever procedures are adopted to meet the needs of gifted children, it is generally agreed that they should be given a broader, deeper, and more challenging education than that provided for the average child. The program must be guided both by the special needs of these children and by the needs of the society in which we live.

In any planning, the gifted child must be considered as a total person, and must be supported and guided without anyone "sitting on" his exuberant efforts. The teacher is in a key position and plays a vital role in discovering and providing for the gifted child in the classroom. The success of any program depends on the teacher, who is the most important facet and instrument of the program.

The administrator serves as the motivator of people (staff, community, students) and the promoter of a practical, flexible, and meaningful program. This may be accomplished by providing ongoing staff training for curriculum development and new trends and methods of teaching the gifted student, as well as through periodic newsletters, newspapers, and parent meetings. It is essential that a mechanism be established to monitor and evaluate the appropriateness and effectiveness of the program so that necessary modifications can be made when needed.

A profusion of studies have moved from a concentration on the nature of giftedness to the multidimensional nature of talent to the identity, selection, and role of the gifted in our schools with greater and clearer concern for programing. By the end of the 1980's we should begin to see definite results of the increasing commitment to development of programs that will with determination become an integral part of the school curriculum. Schools must identify early those children with exceptional abilities and nurture those findings. Early identification of gifted children is important if they are to benefit from special educational programs. Education of the gifted should be a three way partnership of parents, teachers, and community. Such early identification improves the chances for proper challenge and channeling. The need to identify youngsters does not stop here. Evaluation of potential and observation of behavior and achievement should continue throughout school life.

A top priority of the education system must be to sensitize all teachers in their college preparation and on the job training to the multiple nature of giftedness so that they will recognize it when they see it and adapt their instruction accordingly. Under the guidance of teachers who recognize and respect them for the unique people they are, we can do so much for so very little simply by freeing the gifted to grow and develop more fully.

Program planning must be based on the actual needs and interests of the pupil. Freedom from unwarranted restrictions of structured requirements and schedules will provide access to learning resources outside the confines of the school environment. A system is needed in which students are treated as individuals, educated in relation to their potential and unique talents, and prepared as much as possible to meet their present and future needs as persons and as citizens in a democratic society. There is no other societal structure which will more directly help students face their struggles, formulate their aspirations, and hold forth the promise that their hopes can be realized.

CHAPTER 2

Getting Started and Moving into Implementation

WILLIAM G. VASSAR

During the past few years, the education of the gifted and talented has again come to the forefront of thinking in the minds of many professional and lay personnel. Many factors have brought about a rethinking of the needs of our nation's human resources. More students are being recognized for their demonstrated and potential talents; more states and local school districts have taken a greater interest in special programing; and the federal sector has assumed a more active leadership role in establishing such programing as a high priority.

Among those professionals interested in a more coordinated effort between general education and special education for the gifted and talented, the fact should be recognized that every school in the nation has children and youth with demonstrated and/or potential extraordinary ability levels. How classroom teachers, curriculum coordinators, or other professional educators perceive the needs of the gifted and talented, and how they attempt to provide effective programs and services, will be determining factors in how successfully a school district meets those needs.

MEETING THE NEEDS OF GIFTED AND TALENTED STUDENTS

Professional educators should recognize the special needs of the gifted and talented as they do those of other exceptional children. These include the need for:

- Opportunities to understand, develop, and use the higher mental processes associated with high levels of academic and artistic talent.

- Time to meet and interact with their academic, artistic, and leadership peers who have similar interests and talents.
- Time, space, and human resources to assist in the development of an individual talent or ability.
- Opportunities to understand, appreciate, and study the diversity that exists among individuals.
- Availability of an appropriate screening and identification process and access to specialized counseling.
- Development of learning styles and lifestyles commensurate with their particular profile of abilities and talents.
- Opportunities for self assessment of talents and interests.

A special program for *any exceptional child* is basically *one element* of a total design for meeting the needs of individual students or groups of students. It should not be conceived as a program assigning special privileges to a select few for a narrow purpose. Differentiated instruction and administrative designs for the gifted and talented should be articulated and coordinated with all levels of general education and with any other special provisions being implemented in the school district.

Administrative leadership, at all levels, can stimulate identification and programing for gifted and talented students throughout the school district. Instructional and ancillary personnel must be actively and continuously involved in such programing if a district is to provide a meaningful program. Educators should be fully aware of (1) state and federal laws, regulations, and guidelines concerning the gifted and talented; (2) state and federal resources relating to all aspects of the gifted and talented; (3) local policies and position statements; and (4) attitudes of the various publics in the community.

GETTING STARTED—A PLAN OF ACTION

An effective plan of action begins by identifying the need and purposes for special programs and services for the gifted and talented. A planning committee should consider the following sequential stages as they design, develop, and implement programs and services.

Exploratory Stage

1. Establish need for a special program in the district.
2. Make decision to design and develop the special program.
3. Delegate responsibility to Planning and Placement Team (see Chapter 13).
4. Appoint Planning and Placement Team, including representatives from such groups as administrators, pupil personnel and instructional staff, lay persons, parents, and youth.

5. Establish time line for developing program.
6. Develop district position statement on the gifted and talented.
7. Design program purposes that reflect all local and state ramifications.

Initiatory Stage

1. Begin planning district program.
   a. Assess needs of the school district.
   b. Review theories and recent research in the field of gifted and talented.
   c. Survey status of any existing special provisions for the gifted and talented in the district.
2. Define gifted and talented as appropriate for local needs.
   a. Review position statement and purposes previously developed.
   b. Assess local situations, values, attitudes, and political realities.
3. Determine target group(s) and grade level(s) of program.
   a. Study local and state incidence statistics of target group(s).
   b. Review other available state and federal statistical information applicable to local definition.
   c. Identify target group(s) to be served, such as the highly creative or highly motivated.
   d. Determine grade levels to be involved.
   e. Make sure that target group(s) reflect the community's population makeup.
   f. Assess budgetary factors in terms of staff limitations.

Goals and Objectives Stage

1. Synthesize purposes into program goals.
2. Determine student related program goals.
3. Translate program goals to specific objectives.
   a. Develop overall program objectives.
   b. Determine student objectives.
   c. Develop teacher objectives, stated in terms of personal objectives, process objectives, and environment (facilities).
4. Review evaluation processes to measure objectives.

Program Planning Stage

1. Review the target group(s) to be involved in special programs.
2. Review grade levels and number of students to be served.
3. Develop appropriate screening and identification procedures.
   a. Consider characteristics of various types of gifted and talented (high achievers, disadvantaged, underachievers, etc.).
   b. Determine appropriate multiple criteria for selection of program participants.

    c. Review literature, research, and other information to promote appreciation for complexity of the selection process.

    d. Study various types of instrumentation such as tests, checklists, and rating scales.

4. Develop administrative designs for placement of students for instructional purposes.

    a. Select appropriate options in relation to local needs (regular classroom, special classes, resource room, regional approach, itinerant teacher).

    b. Consider transportation, availability of facilities, geography, community feelings and values.

5. Develop strategies for differentiation of instruction.

    a. Determine differentiation of curriculum in terms of workable adaptations, theories, and approaches.

    b. Determine differentiation of teaching strategies appropriate for the target group(s) being served.

    c. Determine level of involvement of community resources, both human and physical.

6. Develop appropriate time frame for student participation in program.

    a. Establish length of time differentiated instruction is needed.

    b. Consider availability of special teachers.

7. Develop plan to articulate and coordinate special programs with general programs and between grade levels and system levels within the district.

Personnel Development Stage

1. Select professional and paraprofessional personnel.

    a. Develop criteria or list of desired characteristics for staff selection.

    b. Design criteria that reflect how personnel will be assigned in instructional or ancillary capacities.

2. Provide opportunities for continuous inservice training for special and general staff.

    a. Design specific training activities.

    b. Identify inservice resources (consultants, materials).

3. Develop training for ancillary staff, including counselors, psychologists, and social workers.

Evaluation and Budgetary Stage

1. Develop plan for evaluation of special programs.

    a. Establish evaluative criteria and communicate these to all staff involved.

    b. Design system for monitoring program.

    c. Develop design for gathering and compiling data relevant to student progress and related program objectives.

d. Determine purposes for evaluation and recipients of evaluation data.
2. Develop program budget.
   a. Instructional staff.
   b. Ancillary staff.
   c. Materials and equipment.
   d. Rental of facilities, if needed.
   e. Inservice training.
   f. Evaluation.
   g. Transportation.
   h. Miscellaneous.

MAINTAINING MOMENTUM

Succeeding chapters in this handbook discuss in detail the key elements of program administration, including screening and identification, aspects of differentiated instruction, budgeting, staffing, program evaluation, involvement of parents and the community, and the unique considerations of the special gifted populations of handicapped and minority students.

Programing for the gifted and talented is an integral part of the total educational process. By their special nature, programs will vary from district to district. To lay a solid foundation, however, exploration of the many aspects of a program for the gifted and talented should be compatible with the following major features of program design.

1. Those involved in the total program should have a thorough knowledge of the broadened concept of giftedness.
2. Curriculum, instructional, and pupil personnel staff should play key roles in designing and developing programs.
3. A needs assessment should be conducted in the school district to identify priority needs of the gifted and talented.
4. The philosophy and objectives for pupils, staff, and program should be clearly established.
5. Identification criteria for the specific target group(s) should be fully developed in accordance with the multiple criteria concept.
6. The administrative design for service should be developed according to local needs.
7. The core of the program should reflect a differentiated curriculum design articulated with differentiated teaching strategies for the gifted and talented.
8. The differentiated program should be articulated and coordinated with total general education at all levels.
9. Public understanding should be nurtured among all community groups.
10. Instructional and support personnel should be carefully selected.

11. A definitive evaluation plan should be developed to assure that the goals for both pupils and program will be met.
12. Parents should play an integral role in all aspects of the program.
13. Community resources, both human and physical, should be fully utilized in program development and implementation.
14. Funding sources from all public and private sectors should be explored.

CHAPTER 3

Policy Implications
for Administrators

JOHN A. GROSSI

Policy makers and implementors are in agreement. To achieve goals and objectives crucial to the successful establishment and operation of any education program, it is imperative that policy delineating purpose and direction be developed and implemented. In the United States, the education of the gifted and talented has suffered from a paucity of programmatic policy at the national, state, and local levels. Only within the last 3 years have gifted and talented children and their education become a major national priority. The US Congress has shown a marked increase in interest and activity in this area of exceptional child education by providing new legislation for the gifted and talented and charging appropriate federal agencies with its regulation and implementation. Persons advocating for improved programing have felt that federal involvement, both in policy and fiscal support, represents a long awaited commitment from this country's legislative body.

HISTORICAL OVERVIEW OF FEDERAL POLICY

School district and building administrators intent on establishing and maintaining programs for gifted and talented students must not only be aware of current federal policy affecting these children, but of previously established policies as well. Because this country's history of educating the gifted and talented has been more passive than in other areas of exceptional child education, it is easy to overlook past activities. Administrators who ignore this past will undoubtedly repeat it, thus running the risk of establishing programs for gifted and talented children that may be doomed to failure.

America's first serious approach to establishing provisions for the education of the gifted and talented was in the late 1950's. America's self image had been tarnished by the launching of the Soviet satellite, Sputnik. Critics blamed America's public education system for our losing the race to space. In response, Congress hastily passed The National Defense Education Act and the National Science Foundation Program. The purpose of these two separate pieces of federal legislation was to provide financial assistance to state and local education agencies for the purpose of creating programs and strategies to help meet the unique educational needs of their gifted and talented students. Some of the more common program options employed as a result of this legislation were honors classes, science and math curricula, early admissions to college, acceleration, and enrichment.

Unfortunately, the impact of such innovative programing was fleeting, for within the next few years America was able to surpass the Russians in aerospace technology, thus eliminating previously expressed fears. In addition, a new administration identified different, more pressing national priorities that shifted public attention from the gifted and talented to the more disadvantaged and impoverished members of our society. It was during this time that programs such as Head Start, VISTA, and the Peace Corps came into existence.

This change in priorities had major implications for both federal and state agencies dealing with the gifted and talented. Many state statutes developed during the earlier peak period never became fully implemented or were overlooked altogether. In addition, federal monies appropriated to establish public school programs for the gifted and talented were being expended in other areas perceived to have more pressing concerns, such as the hiring of guidance counselors and supplementary local school personnel and the purchase of additional audiovisual equipment.

P.L. 91–230, Amendments to the Elementary and Secondary Education Act

Advocates for the gifted and talented continued to bring the needs of these children to the attention of their elected representatives, and in 1969, Congress responded by passing Public Law 91–230, Amendments to the Elementary and Secondary Education Act. The basic intent of this law was to allow gifted and talented students to benefit from existing federal legislation. One option under this authority was for state and local districts to use those funds appropriated under Title III, Supplementary Educational Centers and Services; Guidance, Counseling and Testing; and Title V, Strengthening State and Local Educational Agencies. These allowances provided for the purchase of educational equipment, part time teachers, consultants, coordinators, and technical advisors.

As a result of P.L. 91–230, Congress directed the Commissioner of Education, Sidney Marland, to identify the educational needs of the gifted and talented through a national survey and from collected and analyzed information and to suggest ways in which the federal government might facilitate programs and services to meet those needs.

In the fall of 1971, Commissioner Marland submitted his landmark study to Congress. Marland reported that:

- Only a fraction of the nation's gifted and talented children were actually receiving educational services.
- Services to this population were a low administrative priority.
- Little innovation and accomplishment in the field of gifted and talented education was actually taking place.
- Available federal assistance for the gifted and talented was not being used to the extent anticipated.

Since the Marland report concluded that unspecified federal appropriations were not being used for the gifted and talented, Congress had to devise a new approach that would allow federal assistance and appropriations to directly reach gifted and talented students, agencies, and institutions most concerned with their education.

P.L. 93–380, the Elementary and Secondary Education Act

In 1974, Congress enacted Public Law 93–380, the reauthorization of the Elementary and Secondary Education Act. Section 404 of that law, the "Special Projects Act," paved the way for the gifted and talented to become direct recipients of federal funds and assistance.

Section 404 used the following approach to the delivery of support and advocacy.

- *The Office of Gifted and Talented.* In order to monitor activities and administer programs for the gifted and talented, Congress authorized the Commissioner to establish a national advocacy office. Created in 1972 and housed within the existing Bureau of Education for the Handicapped it came to be known as the Office of Gifted and Talented.
- *National Information Clearinghouse.* To facilitate programs for the gifted and talented, Congress appropriated funds to the National Institute of Education (NIE). In 1972, NIE awarded funds for the purpose of establishing an information clearinghouse for the gifted and talented to The Council for Exceptional Children (CEC), which incorporated this component into its existing Educational Resources Information Center (ERIC) Clearinghouse for the Handicapped.

- *State and Local Education Agencies.* In 1976, Congress appropriated a total of $2.56 million for the gifted and talented, to be awarded to state and local education agencies. The primary purpose of this appropriation was to assist state and local education agencies in the development of planning strategies and the establishment and operation of programs to meet the special educational needs of gifted and talented students.
- *Training, Research, and Model Projects.* Section 404 also addressed the need for training existing and potential leadership personnel involved in the education of the gifted and talented. Leadership training identified by the law included university graduate training programs; leadership training institutes; and federal, state, and local internships. Congress also authorized the establishment of model projects targeted toward distinct components and subpopulations of the gifted and talented.

Title IX and P.L. 95–561

The level and formula of appropriations for the gifted and talented pursuant to Section 404 of P.L. 93–380, remained constant until the reauthorization of the Elementary and Secondary Education Act in 1978. At that time, both professional and advocate groups had, after 5 years of experimentation with gifted and talented education as a "special project," decided that the time had come to remove the authority for gifted and talented from its ancillary placement within the federal bureaucracy and into a more viable statutory program. Again, Congress responded positively with the creation of Title IX, the Education of the Gifted and Talented, and of P.L. 95–561, the Elementary and Secondary Education Act of 1978. Though the purpose of this new legislation was similar to that of preceding federal policy, the focus, formula, and level of appropriations were adjusted.

The purpose of this new federal legislation for the gifted and talented differs from that of P.L. 93–380, in that greater emphasis is placed on assistance to state and local education agencies to develop, implement, and monitor educational programs and services for gifted and talented students. The legislation further directs the Commissioner of Education to use 75% of the total appropriation for grant awards to state education agencies for the support of planning, developing, operating, and improving programs designed to meet the educational needs of gifted and talented children at the preschool, elementary, and secondary levels.

One major aspect of this formula approach is for state education agencies to retain only 10% of their total award. The remaining 90% of the award is earmarked for distribution, on a competitive basis, to local education agencies within each state, highlighting the increased involvement of administrators in their educational program decision making, and facilitation of direct services to gifted and talented students. An additional priority identified in this legislation is the economically disadvantaged gifted and talented student. To achieve the purpose of the law, state education agencies must assure that at least 50% of the monies awarded to local districts are used either to serve economically disadvantaged gifted and talented students directly, or to support programs that will benefit these children.

The remaining 25% of the total federal appropriation is considered discretionary, and is reserved for direct awards to state education agencies, local education agencies, institutions of higher education, and other public and private agencies and institutions. The purpose of the discretionary awards is to assist recipients in establishing or maintaining programs or projects designed to meet the educational needs of gifted and talented children including the training of personnel in educating gifted and talented children or in supervising such personnel. The award options available through the discretionary portion are:

- *Inservice.* "Grants to provide for the training of personnel engaged in the education of gifted and talented children or in the supervision of such children." (Sec. 905[a][2])
- *Model Projects.* "Grants or contracts to establish and operate model projects for the identification and education of gifted and talented children." (Sec. 905[a][3])
- *Clearinghouse.* "Grants or contracts designed to disseminate information about programs, services, resources, research, methodology and media materials for the education of gifted and talented children." (Sec. 905[a][4])
- *Statewide Planning.* "Grants to SEAs to assist them in the statewide planning, development, operation and improvement of programs and projects designed to meet the educational needs of gifted and talented children." (Sec. 905[a][5])
- *Research and Demonstration.* "Research, evaluation and related activities pertaining to the education of gifted and talented children." (Sec. 905[a][6])

Summary Outline of Federal Policy

As a measure to safeguard administrators from making common mistakes concerning programmatic policy, the following outline has been developed to summarize and clarify the history of federal policy affecting the gifted and talented.

I. 1958: National Defense Education Act and National Science Foundation Programs
   Intent: To increase America's technological resources and capacity.
   Execution: The availability of monies through honors programs, innovative math and science curricula, scholarships, early admissions to college, etc.

Impact: Minimal, as public interest shifted and states postponed the implementation of developed laws. Available federal funds were expended on what states considered higher priorities, i.e., school counselors, audiovisual materials, etc.

II. 1969: P.L. 91–230: Elementary and Secondary Education Amendments (Section 806, Provisions Related to Gifted and Talented Children)
   Intent: To demonstrate Congressional desire to educate gifted and talented children and to provide a vehicle for the Commissioner of Education to conduct a study to determine the state of gifted and talented education and to recommend possible federal assistance.
   Execution: The authorization of Titles III and V monies to be used by state and local education agencies for consultants, coordinators, and/or technical advisors, and through the conduction of a Congressional report to determine the state of the art of gifted and talented education.

III. 1974: P.L. 93–380: Amendments to the Elementary and Secondary Education Act (Title IV, the Special Project, Section 404, "Gifted and Talented Children").
   Intent: For gifted and talented children to receive primary focus, and by providing a statutory base for:
   • An administrative unit within the United States Office of Education.
   • The establishment of a national information clearinghouse.
   • Grants to state and local education agencies.
   • Authorization for training, research, and model projects.
   Execution: By implementing each of the major components mentioned above through the appropriation of $2.56 million each year from 1976 to 1978.
   Impact: For the first time, the federal government was able to provide some support to state and local, public and private agencies and institutions in the delivery of educational services to gifted and talented children. Increased activity in this area of exceptional child education provided an increase in public awareness of the needs of these children and provided direction and input for subsequent federal and state legislation.

IV. 1978: P.L. 95–561: The Elementary and Secondary Education Act (Title IX, the Education of the Gifted and Talented).
   Intent: To provide financial assistance to state and local education agencies, institutions of higher education, and other public and private agencies and organizations to assist those agencies in the planning, development, operation, and improvement of programs designed to meet the special educational needs of gifted and talented children.

Execution: Through state education agencies to local education agencies on a competitive basis and through grants and contracts awarded on discretionary funds.

Impact: Still to be determined.

Adapted from Zettel, J. *Federal influence in gifted and talented educational policy development.* Unpublished manuscript, 1976.

INDIVIDUAL STATE POLICIES ON GIFTED AND TALENTED

Although the federal government did not, until recently, provide explicit direction through policy for the gifted and talented, individual states have in many instances taken the lead. In a 1977 survey conducted by The Council for Exceptional Children, each state and territory was asked to describe and document the existence of state policy governing the education of gifted and talented children. This study revealed that 37 states had both statutes and administrative policy (CEC, 1978).

Each state's policy differed according to its priorities. However, all state policy may be grouped into two major categories: *mandation*, which requires that all local education agencies provide educational services to their gifted and talented students; or *permissive*, where local districts have the option of serving gifted and talented students. In 1977, 9 states mandated educational services for the gifted and talented. In 1979, 18 states were mandating. This difference reflects a 100% increase in a span of only 2 years. Therefore, the emerging trend appears to be toward states adopting policy requiring the education of gifted and talented children.

THE ADMINISTRATOR'S ROLE

Though the focal point of most recent policy activity for the gifted and talented has been at the national level, the major responsibility for implementation of policy rests with state and local districts. Pressure to establish education programs for the gifted and talented from parents, educators, policymakers, and other advocates is a present administrative reality. In addition to the responsibilities for designing and maintaining alternative programs for the gifted and talented, administrators should be concerned with local autonomy. Developed policy should provide options that maintain both autonomy and cross district collaboration. Employment of one or the other policy option carries with it certain implications for successful facilitation of education programs for gifted and talented children.

To be most effective, policy should provide direction, authority, and guidelines for establishing programs. Administrators are responsible for interpreting that policy and applying it to their districts. To assist in the process, administrators may wish to undertake the following sequential steps:

- *Assemble policy material.* The extent of local programing for the gifted and talented often depends on federal, state, and local legislation, regulations, guidelines, etc., which authorize and support such programing. To be most knowledgeable about policies affecting the gifted and talented, administrators should assemble and become familiar with all existing policy material and information. This knowledge will facilitate progress in the appropriate direction and assure that both the locus and focus of those efforts are pursuant to established policy.
- *Conduct work sessions.* As the primary facilitator of district efforts, the administrator is responsible for conducting work sessions concerning the formulation of programs to include policy elements and decisions on alternative approaches to programing. Those approaches may expand on established policy guidelines, but should not be less than is specified.
- *Draft and revise proposal.* Once a decision has been made as to the type and extent of district programing for the gifted and talented, the administrator should develop a draft program proposal for review by appropriate personnel. Input received should be incorporated into subsequent drafts until all parties involved are satisfied that the potential program will meet the needs of students, their parents, and administrators. State and local policy statements that provide the authority for what is proposed should be included.
- *Obtain fiscal support.* If fiscal support for the program is being sought from either inside or outside sources, appropriate forms and guidelines should be obtained, completed, and submitted with the program proposal to the funding agency.
- *Begin program implementation.* Once funding has been secured, the administrator must begin the process of program implementation which includes staffing, student selection, curriculum development, etc. Again, established policy should provide the guidelines in such areas as staffing and student identification.
- *Promote public awareness.* To assure maximum exposure for the program and to solicit community and state involvement, administrators should undertake activities to make the public aware of the program, authorizing policies, funding sources, goals, objectives, and, if appropriate, anticipated results and/or end products.
- *Conduct evaluation.* Evaluation should be conducted at each program level where objectives were established. Each objective should be written in measurable terms or should cite the instrument that will be used in the evaluation of that objective. Both cognitive and affective assessments should be made in order to view the program from several perspectives.

Evaluation can be either formative or summative. In the former approach, data is collected throughout the operation of the program in order to point out areas that may need modifications, while in the latter, evaluation takes place at the conclusion of the program and determines end results. A combination of both types has proved to be most successful.

POLICY ISSUES FOR THE 1980's

As the education of the gifted and talented progresses into the 1980's, administrators must be cognizant of those policy issues that will be explored and decided in the decade to come. In the past, there has been a paucity of educational program policy for the gifted and talented. In many instances programs for the gifted and talented have had to operate under policies developed for other populations.

If administrators are to assist in furthering the education of the gifted and talented, they must not be content to allow others outside this content area to determine what that education should entail. Rather, administrators should face the issues surrounding the education of the gifted and talented and address each of them by assisting in the development and implementation of state and local policy that will have a positive impact on gifted education.

Policy issues to be addressed and questions to be answered by administrators in the 1980's include the following:

1. Definition of the gifted and talented
   a. Does my state or local district have a definition of the gifted and talented?
   b. Are existing federal and state definitions adequate for use in my district?
   c. Are they too broad? Too narrow?
   d. Does the existing definition in place in my state or district assist in the identification process?

2. Identification of gifted and talented students
   a. Does my state or district have procedures to locate, assess, and identify gifted and talented students?
   b. Does my state or district have administrative guidelines governing the assessment and determination of eligibility of gifted and talented students for special programing?
   c. Does my state or district have assessment materials and procedures to be used during the identification process that will assure that gifted

and talented students are selected in a nondiscriminatory fashion as to race, color, religion, creed, national origin, sex, or handicapping condition?

d. Is my state or district sure to use multiple criteria either for determining an appropriate educational program for gifted and talented students or for denying placement to those students?

e. Does my state or local district have administrative guidelines governing the types of assessment materials and procedures that a school district may use?

3. Service delivery
   a. Does my state or district have guidelines for the development and implementation of an individually designed education program for the gifted and talented?
   b. Does my school district insure that alternative education provisions for gifted and talented students are available as necessary?

4. Procedural safeguards
   a. Has my state or district informed parents of gifted and talented students of their rights to have access to their child's school records?
   b. Does my state or district have in place a procedure for conducting due process hearings?

5. Administration
   a. Does my state or district have an office or division to administer programs for the gifted and talented?
   b. Is there a sufficient number of personnel in my state or local district to enable the state or local district to carry out effective programing for the gifted and talented?
   c. Does my state or local district have an advisory council to advise and consult with state and local personnel about the education of the gifted and talented?
   d. Does my state and local district keep and make current a plan for the implementation of a program for the gifted and talented?

6. School district responsibility
   a. Does my district have a person to coordinate local efforts on behalf of the gifted and talented?
   b. Does my district conduct a survey on a regular basis to determine the number of gifted and talented students in the district?
   c. Does my district use survey information to assist in future planning for the gifted and talented?
   d. Has my district developed a plan to facilitate an appropriate education for the gifted and talented?

LOOKING AHEAD

As the education of exceptional children expands, administrators will be exploring alternative options for providing these children with an appropriate education in the context of existing and future laws. Developing policy that establishes the environment for the education of exceptional children, including the gifted and talented, is fast becoming an additional administrative responsibility. Serious attention to policy development is therefore a prerequisite for the administrator of the 1980's.

REFERENCES

The Council for Exceptional Children. *The nation's commitment to the education of gifted and talented children and youth: Summary of findings from a 1977 survey of states and territories.* Reston VA: The Council for Exceptional Children, 1978.

Grossi, J. A. *Model state policy, legislation and state plan toward the education of gifted and talented students: A handbook for state and local districts.* Reston VA: The Council for Exceptional Children, 1980.

Title IX: Gifted and talented children's education act of 1978. Reston VA: The Council for Exceptional Children, 1978.

CHAPTER 4

Needs Assessment

JOYCE VAN TASSEL

Traditionally, the definition of needs assessment has been the determination of the difference between the actual and preferred status of a given entity, with the implication being that the gap or discrepancy between these two states should be the focus of program action. More recently, Dr. Michael Scriven of the Evaluation Institute at the University of San Francisco has called need "a factor without which an entity would not function satisfactorily." Scriven's pragmatic definition further states that need does not obligate action. Setting priorities, effecting compromise, and working out a budget based on available funds are all activities that must be taken into account in formal needs assessment processes.

Both definitions are relevant to program planning in gifted education. While the approach to assessment may focus on discrepancy, the Scriven definition can be used to assess the extent of program development to be effected any given year in a school district or state. At any rate, understanding needs and documenting them is a necessary starting point for looking at program development in gifted education.

MAJOR COMPONENTS OF A NEEDS ASSESSMENT

In order to begin planning a gifted program, educators must first conceptualize the need for such a program. At the federal level, the need has been well documented in the Marland report (1972) which noted that less than 4% of the nation's gifted youngsters were being served in special programs, that 55% were underachievers, and that 14% of one state's dropouts had IQ's of 130 and above. These data certainly reflect one kind of need.

Another level of needs assessment should occur, however, at the local level in order to determine what currently exists for gifted students and what needs to exist. This task can be accomplished through asking students, parents, administrators, teachers, and others to comment formally on this aspect of the district's educational plan. Once it has been ascertained that a percentage of the district's gifted population is not receiving services or that existing services are not adequate to the needs, then the mechanism is in place to begin formal program planning.

How can a needs assessment be done? What are its most important components? It is useful to start with a list of questions which can be answered by a good needs assessment.

1. Based on the characteristics of gifted children in this district, what are the educational needs for which we are responsible?
2. What are the gaps in our current program which need to be addressed in order to provide appropriate intervention for gifted students?
3. What kinds of technical assistance do we need in order to proceed with program development?

Thus, to ascertain needs in gifted education, it is first necessary to delineate significant areas from which information must be gleaned. These need areas include students, programs, and technical assistance as it relates to consultation and training. Within these need areas are several important considerations to be examined in the development of a program model.

1. The concept of student needs can be explored through the aggregation of characteristics cited in research filtered through practical considerations in programing.
2. The concept of program needs should reflect a concern for the disparity between the actual and preferred state in a close examination of each major component of a gifted program.
3. The concept of technical assistance is a developmental phenomenon and therefore dynamic rather than static, a natural outgrowth of planning decisions rather than an end in itself.
4. Technical assistance should evolve from program needs which in turn emanate from student needs. Thus, a cyclical model which recognizes these relationships should be developed.
5. The recycling phase of the model is a critical consideration as planning occurs from year to year.

The model presented on p. 25 delineates areas of needs, their component parts, and the interrelationships of each to the other.

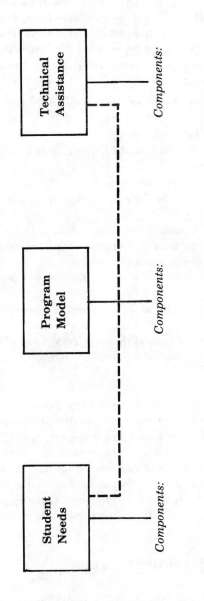

A CYCLICAL NEEDS IDENTIFICATION MODEL

Student Needs

Components:

A. Cognitive
B. Affective

Program Model

Components:

A. Human Resources
B. Structure/Organization
C. Content
D. Instructional Strategies
E. Developmental Concerns

Technical Assistance

Components:

A. Resources (human and material)
B. Time
C. Mode

DETERMINATION OF STUDENT NEEDS

In order to plan effective special programs for gifted students, school districts must understand the special needs of the population involved. Currently, documentation of needs may be available from information contained in the individualized education program (IEP) and other assessment forms at the local district level. However, because of the rudimentary state of such documents at this time, a student needs list has been compiled.

Gifted and talented students need:

1. Activities that enable them to operate cognitively and affectively at complex levels of thought and feeling.
2. Opportunities for divergent production.
3. Challenging group and individual work which demonstrates process/product outcomes.
4. Discussions among intellectual peers.
5. A variety of experiences that promote understanding of human value systems.
6. The opportunity to see interrelationships in all bodies of knowledge.
7. Special courses in their area of strength and interest which accelerate the pace and depth of the content.
8. Greater exposure to new areas of learning within and outside the school structure.
9. Opportunities to apply their abilities to real problems in the world of production.
10. To be taught the skills of critical thinking, creative thinking, research, problem solving, coping with exceptionality, decision making, and leadership.

This needs list can be used by districts in three major ways to document their student needs. First, districts could prioritize this list of needs according to the percent of students demonstrating each of them, and according to the degree of each need (mild, moderate, severe) as ascertained by professional staff. Second, districts may use the list as a student survey in current gifted programs to ascertain what needs gifted students feel are being met and which ones are not. Finally, districts may aggregate the top need areas and translate them into major program objectives.

DETERMINATION OF PROGRAM NEEDS

Delineation of the following program components reflects an attempt to present several alternatives necessary to effect a gifted program at the local level, regardless of grade level or other arbitrary designation. Data gathered from specific existing programs in gifted education were used to compile each component list. Form 1 at the end of this chapter offers a survey format for assessing general program needs.

Human Resource Alternatives

All gifted programs must use personnel in various configurations in order to function. The use of a variety of personnel is essential to provide a comprehensive programing effort. Listed below are personnel used in successful gifted programs and the role that each performs. A district should decide at the needs assessment phase which of these human resource alternatives are essential for the implementation of their gifted program.

- *Teachers:* Act as instructors, counselors, facilitators, and advisors for programs.
- *Outside Consultants:* Assist in inservice, planning, and demonstration teaching.
- *Parents:* Help with field trips; act as guest lecturers; work as aides or classroom volunteers.
- *Administrators:* Develop and implement the program, acting as fiscal agents and decision makers.
- *Students:* Function as the target group for programs; tutor younger gifted children; work as mentors.
- *Community Volunteers:* Work as teachers in a program once or twice a week; act as guides for out of school experiences.
- *Psychologists/Diagnostic Personnel:* Handle all testing and identification protocol for the program; hold conferences with parents and teachers.
- *Social Workers:* Work with gifted children experiencing home problems.
- *Guidance Counselors:* Work with gifted children in areas such as coping with giftedness, career education, psychosocial concerns.

Structural Alternatives

All gifted programs operate in an administrative configuration, including elements such as teaching arrangement, facilities, a time frame, and grouping procedures. The chart on p. 28 shows the most common administrative alternatives to implementing a gifted program. A good needs assessment asks significant publics to select an alternative that is consonant with their philosophical beliefs about the gifted and affords the best setting to meet the needs of these students.

Content Alternatives

Regardless of the overall program configuration, all gifted programs must offer a base of content. Deciding on which area or areas will be covered is

ALTERNATIVE ADMINISTRATIVE ARRANGEMENTS

Grouping Procedures: IEP's in regular classroom.	*Grouping Procedures:* Pull-out program, mixed grade grouping, grades 3–5.	*Grouping Procedures:* Cluster grouping of gifted students, grades 2–3 in one third grade classroom (other students also assigned).	*Grouping Procedures:* Separate class/course for identified students, grades 7–8.
Frequency of Contact: 150 minutes per week for each identified student.	*Frequency of Contact:* 1 hour per day (300 minutes per week).	*Frequency of Contact:* All day.	*Frequency of Contact:* 1 hour per day.
Site: Every school, all classrooms, grades 4–6.	*Site:* Each school's resource room.	*Site:* One school, primary level.	*Site:* Junior high classroom.
Teaching Arrangement: All teachers, grades 4–6, plan together once a week for gifted students and arrange for group contact time.	*Teaching Arrangement:* Itinerant teacher works with identified students on preassigned schedule.	*Teaching Arrangement:* One primary teacher works with gifted students on an ongoing basis.	*Teaching Arrangement:* One junior high teacher works with identified students as part of regular class load.

a critical part of planning. Student needs data should be used to make decisions in this area as well. Common content alternatives in gifted education include:

Reading	Music	Philosophy
Language Arts	Career	Creative Writing
Mathematics	Education	Leadership
Science	Humanities	Creative Thinking
Social Studies	Speech	Critical Thinking
Foreign Language	Dramatics	Independent
Art	Logic	Research Projects

A needs assessment attempts to seek input regarding those content areas where the greatest gaps in programing seem to exist for the gifted students in a given district. By including choices that may not currently be offered, but that have proven to be effective in programs for the gifted, program planners can broaden the vistas of thinking about program options.

Instructional Strategy Alternatives

A wide variety of teaching strategies used in gifted programs can be examined for purposes of assessing program needs, including:

Lecture	Experiential (classroom/
Group Discussion	laboratory based)
Independent Study	Materials Utilization
Modeling/Demonstration	Practicum (community based)
Simulations/Games	Drill and Recitation
Programed Instruction	Peer Projects
Inquiry	Problem Solving (creative/critical)

These strategies should be assessed in light of the nature of the program being planned and the frequency with which gifted students currently experience them. Intelligent choices can be made from such comparisons for inclusion in the program.

Developmental Concerns

The final area for consideration in assessing program needs relates to generic areas of program development, those areas of concern which all program persons must address as they attempt to create a gifted program. A good needs assessment must take into account the areas of program development that need the most work and have the highest priority for the largest number of respondents so that adequate inservice work or consultative sessions can be scheduled. While it can be argued that all of the following core concerns must be addressed, the focus and stress placed on each of them can best be determined through a formal needs assessment.

- Identifying students based on available population assessment data.
- Diagnosing and prescribing for student needs.
- Selecting among alternative program models.
- Delineating the conceptual framework of the program (e.g., Bloom's taxonomy, Structure of the Intellect) through written goals, objectives, and activities.
- Operationalizing the program by means of a written plan through concern for resource allocation, scheduling, curriculum, and materials development.
- Effecting change by working with parents and community, as well as by developing communication skills, consultation skills, and classroom management skills.
- Measuring the success of the program through an evaluation design.
- Recycling the program based on best available data.

DETERMINATION OF TECHNICAL ASSISTANCE NEEDS

Once student needs and program needs have been ascertained, priority areas can be aggregated for decision making in the area of technical assistance. Form 2 at the end of this chapter offers one approach to assessing training needs. The final section of Form 3 (pp. 36–37) illustrates the variety of delivery modes that can properly be termed *technical assistance*. These include seminars, workshops, conferences, team consultation, individual consultation, observation/demonstration, materials, other communications (letters, phone calls, etc.), and college courses. The form also delineates three target areas of change and growth in which all of technical assistance operates: knowledge, skills, and attitudes. This section of Form 3 can be completed by gifted coordinators for each program aspect they identify as a priority area.

NEEDS ASSESSMENT PROCESS

This needs assessment approach represents an attempt to provide gifted educators with a framework around which program planning can occur. It is important to remember, however, that the process employed to gather needs assessment information is as important as the idea and the instrument, perhaps more so. Major steps to consider in conducting a needs assessment are as follows:

1. A committee of program planners with appropriate input from groups they represent should handle the data collection activities through the use of a formal instrument or an agreed upon approach.

2. Program planners should orient groups to the needs assessment process in group meetings rather than by a mailing.
3. Input from a variety of groups should be sought, including students, teachers, administrators, parents, and pupil personnel workers.
4. A check should be made for discrepancies in perceived needs of the various publics responding. If a discrepancy occurs, a decision should be made about the direction of the issue in question.
5. Program decisions should be made based on the general direction indicated by the assessment information, along with the knowledge of what constitutes "best practices" in the field of gifted education.

SUMMARY

The use of a sound needs assessment approach should provide significant benefits to program planners. The student data should provide a sound foundation on which to generate program goals and objectives. The program data should provide helpful information on where the gaps are in program development and what alternatives are preferred in building a complete program. The technical assistance data should provide the basis for a sound, sequential, and ongoing staff development program. Thus, school districts and state agencies can truly participate in comprehensive planning in gifted education. The following sample instruments may be used to facilitate the overall process. They have been field tested at local and state levels.

FORM 1
Needs Assessment for Gifted Program

_____ Check One: _____ Student

Name   _____ Administrator

                                              _____ Teacher

                                              _____ Parent

1. What information needs do you have about gifted education?

2. What form of grouping for the program would you support?

   _____ Separate school
   _____ Fulltime in each school
   _____ Academic subjects only
   _____ Parttime in selected areas
   _____ Only in the regular classroom

3. What content areas do you feel the gifted program should address?

   _____ Reading
   _____ Math
   _____ Social Studies
   _____ Science
   _____ Language Arts
   _____ Music
   _____ Art
   _____ Other (please specify)

4. Who should work with these students?

   _____ Specially trained teachers
   _____ Regular classroom teachers
   _____ Parents
   _____ Community volunteers

5. What should gifted children derive from participation in the program?

6. What other suggestions do you have for developing a new gifted program?

FORM 2
An Assessment of Training Needs

Name: _____

School District Name and Number: _____

Telephone: _____

Please check services you would like to receive from the Area Service Center this coming year:

_____ District inservice workshops

_____ Consultation with gifted committee

_____ Individual consultation on program development

_____ Materials

_____ Demonstration teaching

_____ Exemplary program models (references)

Other services desired (please specify):

What major topics would you like to see covered at regional workshops?

What consultants in gifted education would you like to see present material?

Other suggestions for this year:

FORM 3
A Sample Instrument to Assess Technical Assistance Needs in Gifted Education

The following instrument should be used to assess technical assistance needs in your gifted program based on the past school year. These data will be used by your Area Service Center in developing their work scope for the following year.

Please note the following as you complete the instrument:

1. Get input from as many individuals involved with the program as possible. For example, have your gifted committee fill it out.

2. Check as many areas as you feel are needed, but be sure to prioritize your top *five* choices on the last page.

3. Return the completed instrument to your Area Service Center no later than _____ .

Your cooperation in completing this instrument is sincerely appreciated.

Content Areas	Priority Areas for Technical Assistance (Rank 1–24)		
Humanities		Music	
Reading (K-12)		Performing Arts	
Language Arts (K-8)		Leadership	
English (9-12)		Creativity (writing)	
Mathematics (K-6)		Creativity (thinking)	
Mathematics (7-12)		Critical Thinking	
Science (K-6)		Independent Projects	
Science (7-12)		Logic	
Social Studies (K-6)		Law	
Social Studies (7-12)		Philosophy	
Foreign Language		Psychology	
Art		Career Education	

Utilization of Human Resources	*Priority Areas (Rank 1–5)*
How to utilize community volunteers in a gifted program	
How to utilize psychologists in a gifted program	
How to utilize counselors in a gifted program	
How to utilize parents in a gifted program	
How to utilize_____ in a gifted program	

Organization	*Priority Areas (Rank 1-4)*
A comparison of program organization models in terms of setting and time constraints	
Running off-campus gifted programs	
How to group gifted students	
How to structure a counseling component for the gifted	

Program Development Concerns	*Priority Areas (Rank 1–8)*
Identification based on available student population assessment data	
Diagnosing and prescribing for student needs	
Selecting among alternative program models	
Delineating the conceptual framework of the program (e.g. Bloom's taxonomy) via written goals, objectives, activities	
Operationalizing the program via a written plan, e.g., classroom management skills, resource allocation, scheduling/time management, curriculum, materials development	
Effecting change, e.g., working with parents/ community, communication skills, consultation skills	
Measuring the success of the program via an evaluation design	
Revision and modification based on evaluation/research data	

FORM 3 (continued)

Instructional Strategies	Priority Areas (Rank 1–13)
Lecture	
Group discussion	
Independent study	
Modeling/ Demonstrations	
Simulations/Games	
Programed Instruction	
Inquiry	
Experiential (classroom/laboratory based)	
Materials Utilization	
Practicum (community based)	
Drill and Recitation	
Peer Projects	
Problem Solving (creative/critical)	

Please prioritize your technical assistance choices from the preceding pages and list them in the spaces provided below. Indicate the mode of preferred delivery in columns 1–10 by coding change expectations according to K for knowledge, S for skills, and A for attitudes.

_____

_____

_____

_____

_____

_____

_____

_____

_____

_____

_____

_____

_____

_____

_____

	Seminars	Workshops	Conferences	Team Consultation	Individual Consultation	Observation/Demonstration	Materials	Other Communications	College Courses	Other

CHAPTER 5

Principles of Differentiation of Instruction

JOHN A. GROSSI

At the core of any program for the gifted is the concept of differentiation of instruction. This is probably the most important component of a special program for the gifted and talented. If the approach continues the route of "more of the same," "enrichment undefined," or "expediency acceleration," the program may be doomed to failure (Vassar, 1979).

Key elements are the differentiated curriculum and differentiated teaching strategies. Curriculum designs stress originality, fluency of ideas, intellectual curiosity, independence of thought, and conceptual elaboration. The teaching staff must be trained and skilled in instructional strategies that stress the thinking and feeling processes of analysis and synthesis.

CLARIFYING THE CONCEPT OF DIFFERENTIATION

Special educators involved in the education of the gifted and talented have commonly defined differentiation as the means or *modus operandi* by which a gifted or talented student is allowed to interact with a curriculum to achieve established educational goals and objectives.

At present, there is some confusion regarding the differences between curriculum and differentiation. Many implementors use the terms interchangeably, thus causing difficulty at both administrative and teaching levels. Curriculum and differentiation may perhaps be viewed more clearly as two distinct parts of a whole. For this purpose it would be appropriate to say that curriculum refers to the content to be learned, while differentiation refers to the processes which facilitate that learning.

CURRICULUM FOR THE GIFTED

Gifted and talented students require opportunities which encourage the development of abstract thinking and the sharpening of reasoning abilities. They also require practice in creative problem solving, information analysis, and synthesis and evaluation of that information. Curricula for the gifted and talented therefore often include activities which focus on the interpretation of material being investigated, the development of summative skills, and outlets for creative expression.

While instructional units may be similar for both the gifted and talented and children in regular classrooms, the breadth, depth, and intensity of learning activities within the gifted and talented curriculum mark it as distinctive (CEC, 1978). Teachers are usually responsible for the design and implementation of curriculum for their gifted and talented students. However, students can also share in this responsibility. It is important to emphasize that curriculum for these students should not be a predetermined route which all must follow. Curriculum is a framework for individual learning alternatives. As such, it should be flexible enough to meet the needs of both students and teachers.

The most desirable curriculum is one which fits the learning modes of individual students. It should allow students the opportunity both to create and to consume learning, as well as offer alternative activities for achieving learning objectives. For many gifted and talented students in the regular classroom, the opportunity to receive these considerations is often denied because of the heterogeneous nature of the class and the restraints such heterogeneity places on the teacher.

Because the range of student abilities found in the regular classroom is so diverse, teachers are often forced to gear their activities to those students who run the greatest risk of failure. This approach applies not only to teaching strategies, but to methodologies as well. Teachers may therefore reject approaches which would allow students with different ability levels, such as the gifted and talented, to obtain greater comprehension of subject matter. Differentiation of instruction, if carefully planned and executed, will offer many instructional options to help teachers achieve a greater degree of flexibility in their classrooms and meet the needs of gifted and talented students more effectively.

MAJOR CATEGORIES OF DIFFERENTIATION

Differentiation enhances curriculum. Administrators should present the concept to teachers, parents, and other personnel as a means of allowing students greater challenge in their learning experiences. Although a number of types of differentiation are practical for organizational purposes, the broad categories of acceleration, enrichment, and self contained classrooms (grouping) are conceptually useful. Increased knowledge of these major categories will assist in solving inherent logistical, personnel, and budgetary problems.

Acceleration

For many years, acceleration was viewed as one of the most viable instructional alternatives for use with gifted and talented students. It has also represented one of the more controversial of differentiated approaches to the instruction of the gifted and talented. Until recently, acceleration was viewed solely as removing a child from one school grade to another which was chronologically advanced. This practice, commonly referred to as "skipping," was a popular option of differentiation.

However, both educators and parents have become concerned with potential psychological and educational problems resulting from this type of acceleration. Research has revealed that the cause of such problems was the child's inability to function adequately on a physical and psychological level with children who were more chronologically advanced. Classroom peers mentally placed the gifted child at the lower end of the established pecking order, and the resulting negative school experiences culminated in academic underachievement and/or failure.

The work of Dr. Sanford J. Cohen of Johns Hopkins University has been instrumental in expanding the concept of acceleration by creating other viable instructional possibilities. According to Dr. Cohen, accelerated students are not necessarily harmed emotionally. In fact, nonaccelerated gifted students are often frustrated by the slower learning pace expected of regular classrooms. This frustration also contributes to emotional and academic problems (Cohen, 1979).

An administrator considering the use of acceleration carefully explores the total concept and provides for staff and parent training in its proper use. Rationale for the use of acceleration should include the expected benefits both for students and for the school district. Grade and/or instructional acceleration may enable the gifted and talented student to enter the professional world earlier. The student will also be able to delve into a given curriculum area in greater depth, thus enlarging the knowledge base and providing a greater opportunity for productivity. For the administrator, acceleration often results in lower costs for both the individual and the school, as less time is required to go through the academic system. It has been estimated that acceleration may save an individual $7,500 in costs and may add $10,000 in potential earnings (Jackson & Robinson, 1977).

If used properly, acceleration is one of the more viable of instructional options. Special attention should be given to modifying a curriculum to meet the individual needs of each gifted child who is accelerated. If curriculum modification is not undertaken, one runs the risk of designing a curriculum for older children rather than an appropriate curriculum for gifted students (Renzulli, 1975).

Enrichment

Enrichment opportunities provide the student with experiences not usually encountered in the ongoing school curriculum. In the regular classroom, enrichment often takes an "arts and crafts" approach and may not bear a strong relationship to a student's course of studies. For the gifted and talented, enrichment takes on quite a different guise. While enrichment for the gifted and talented may include arts and crafts, or similar activities, it is by no means limited to this area. Because enrichment should be used to supplement the ongoing curriculum, experiences should be included that provide an opportunity to gain more insight and knowledge of specific discipline areas and topics under study.

Student interest plays a major role in the development and implementation of an enrichment program. A student with high ability in math, for example, may possess the skills and interest necessary to explore and master an area of algebra that his grade peers may not be ready to pursue. An enrichment program, if designed correctly, can respond to this student's interest and readiness and provide the opportunity for intensive investigation.

If no enrichment opportunities exist, the teacher may wish to use a system of student contracts. Independent study projects will stimulate student interest while assuring an orderly sequence of learning experiences. Enrichment possibilities are endless. However, administrators must promote awareness of the techniques of enrichment among teachers and other personnel to assure a steady focus on the hierarchical development of skills and abilities through appropriate challenge to their students.

Self Contained Classrooms

The self contained classroom is by no means a new concept. Self contained classes for the gifted and talented are one of the oldest methods of differential instruction used with this population. Approaches to this instructional alternative fluctuate between inter and extra classroom situations while using one or more instructional options. Simply put, a self contained classroom is any homogeneous grouping of children. Obviously, any homogeneous group is also heterogeneous, as no group of individuals consistently functions at the same cognitive, affective, or psychomotor level. However, a self contained classroom for the gifted and talented places identified students in one location at the same time. This approach facilitates the organization, design, and delivery of special instruction.

From an administrative perspective, the use of a self contained classroom is viable for a number of reasons. Fiscally, it may be less costly. Children are not required to leave the school facility for instruction. Staff requirements are minimal. A self contained classroom may be staffed by one or more present building teachers. Administrators must provide such staff with opportunities that will build their skills and knowledge base. Most importantly, greater benefits for gifted and talented students accrue. The continuity of learning is less dependent on external variables such as logistics and resources, allowing for more contact with instructional personnel and peers of similar ability.

The use of self contained classrooms has met with some resistance. Some educators feel that this approach severely curtails the creativity of both student and teacher. The highly structured format is often believed to curtail the inquiry and discovery operations employed by many gifted and talented children in the learning process. However, the success of this form of differentiation, like others, depends on the learning style of the students, the established need for structure, and the selective use of instructional strategies.

Research on the use of self contained classrooms is inconclusive. While some studies indicate that self contained classrooms have worth, research places the lion's share of responsibility for the success of self contained classrooms on administrators. The indication is that if no curricular modifications are initiated by administrators there will be no change in student behavior (Martinson, 1972). Therefore, administrators should consider the use of self contained classrooms only if they are prepared to contribute adequate time and energy to its success.

RELATED APPROACHES

Other commonly used methods of differentiation for gifted and talented students may be incorporated within the three categories previously described. These include mentorships, internships, the resource room, and the itinerant teacher.

Mentorships

When home and school are unable to provide advanced instruction in a particular curricular area, a common response is to assume that resources are not available and to ignore that portion of the child's curriculum. However, individuals in the local community can often meet the educational needs of these students. The likelihood of the student and the potential resource making contact depends largely upon the organization and coordination necessary to initiate and maintain that contact.

A mentor is a person possessing a particular skill and level of knowledge much greater than the student, and who serves as guide, teacher, advisor, and role model for the student. A comparison may be drawn from the historical master/apprentice relationship, where a young person trained with an expert craftsman for the sole purpose of learning that craft and carrying on its skills and tradition. A true mentorship for the gifted and talented, however, goes much deeper. The mentor often communicates a philosophy of life closely related to an area of high interest in the student's own life. Although this aspect of the mentorship cannot be planned or predetermined, the basic concept remains valid as an approach to meeting the special needs of the gifted and talented.

Advantages of the Program

A community mentorship program offers the opportunity for indepth involvement not possible in a school classroom. It provides the gifted and talented student a learning environment that fosters curiosity and elicits encouragement and response from adults. The challenge offered by the mentor will also test the limits of the student's understanding and skills. For students from ethnic minorities and economically disadvantaged environments, a mentorship may provide the opportunity for recognition that often is overlooked in schools which lack appropriate resources (Boston, 1978).

A mentorship program is not necessarily appropriate for all gifted and talented students. At the elementary school level, a mentorship may not be the most workable option. However, secondary school students who are exploring possible career options, or who have specialized interests and hobbies, may be good candidates for such a program. Students who participate in the program should be mature enough to fulfill their responsibilities in a one to one relationship in order to reap optimum benefits. Part of this maturity is the ability to take criticism, accept guidance, and peruse new areas (Boston, 1978). Most importantly, a mentorship should be viewed as a shared understanding of tasks and responsibilities for both student and mentor (National Commission on Resources for Youth, 1977). This can best be accomplished through the careful matching of student and mentor by a person in the district or school assigned coordinating and maintenance responsibilities.

Role and Function of the Mentorship Coordinator

Administrators responsible for identifying a coordinator should develop a specific job description for that position. The most effective coordinator is one who is familiar with the community and its resources, both human and nonhuman. This person will assist students in the identification of their personal goals in order to facilitate an appropriate student/mentor match. The coordinator is also responsible for surveying the community in search of potential mentors. Interviews should assess the mentors' ability to relate to young people, and should identify their personal goals in the mentorship process. Both student and mentor should find the relationship rewarding, worthwhile, and successful. The coordinator should assist all parties in clarifying their expectations of the experience.

The coordinator should establish two pools of individuals, one of students and one of mentors, in order to begin the tasks of combining interests, abilities, skills, and resources as well as scheduling and transportation to accomplish appropriate student/mentor matches. Obviously, the mentor is the pivotal person in this process. An appropriate mentor generally has the following characteristics:

- Usually but not always an adult.
- Has a special skill, interest, or activity which engages the learner's interest.
- Able to guide the learner toward personally rewarding experiences where challenges can be met, skills developed, problems solved, and relationships established.
- Is flexible, helping the learner review and revise activities and, when necessary, goals.
- Is often a role model for the learner. The mentor can impart an understanding of life styles and attitudes different from those the student might ordinarily meet.
- Is above all interested in the student as a learner and as an individual. (National Commission on Resources for Youth, 1977)

Selecting Mentors

Having identified desired characteristics, the actual selection of mentors can begin. Administrators should assess both the goals of the mentorship program and the resources of the community in which it will operate. Community agencies (governmental, educational, and service) are usually excellent places to start, since these agencies often compile lists of individuals who act as resources in their particular occupational areas. Labor, business, industry, and professional groups may be approached, as well as individual artists, doctors, lawyers, and craftsmen. Selected mentors should reflect not only the obvious characteristics of the community, but its hidden talents as well.

There is no ideal formula for designing a mentorship program. To a large extent, the nature of the community and its resources will determine the shape of a program. However diverse, all mentorship programs should provide opportunities for gifted and talented students to:

- Pursue their interests at an appropriate level of difficulty.
- Explore career options through experience with the real world of work.
- Determine which of many talents and abilities holds the most promise for developing a career or life interest.
- Interact with other highly talented peers and adults. (Hirsch, 1979)

Eliciting Community Support

To gather support for program goals, an administrator may wish to consider making presentations to community groups, parents, school personnel, and other likely sources for mentors. Inform them that mentorship services need not be secured through a programmatic approach but can be established on an individual basis. Factors for administrators to consider as they seek community support include the following:

- A mentorship program can bring the school and the community together.
- Student work habits will be developed and strengthened.
- The innovative nature of the program can be used to generate educator interest.
- The program is not unstructured, but rather seeks to restructure the educational context.
- The program must be carefully evaluated. (National Commission on Resources for Youth, 1977)

Evaluation

Like any education program, a mentorship program should be evaluated on the basis of what it set out to do and how well it was accomplished. Evaluation should assist in making the program better and more effective. Planning for evaluation should begin at the same time as planning for the program itself. Evaluation as an afterthought is usually too little and too late. It seldom provides the opportunity to make timely adjustments during the course of a program's life (Renzulli, 1975).

Internships

The use of internships is more prevalent at the secondary level, primarily because of the responsibilities assumed by the student and the logistics involved in its implementation. An internship experience for a gifted and talented student permits an exploration of the world of work. Extended periods of time are spent with persons, agencies, and institutions implementing tasks required to accomplish specific outcomes in a student's area(s) of interest. Exposure to on the job responsibilities and actually assuming specific work tasks will provide the student with information about a particular profession beyond that included in the regular school curriculum.

Internships may be designed to release the student from attending school for a period of the day, every day, or some portion of the school week. Each scheduling option requires flexibility on the part of the school and school system. Administrators undertaking internship programs for the gifted and talented must be aware of the time, staff, and fiscal requirements involved, and work through any potential problem areas. Internship programs will place the community and the school face to face with the gifted and talented program. It is therefore important that students chosen as interns and the agencies selected to receive them be responsible. The criteria for selecting mentors and students presented in the previous section are also applicable here.

The Resource Room

The resource room is a classroom within a school designed to serve gifted and talented children from within that school for a specified period of time during the student's day or week. Attendance in the resource room is scheduled on a regular basis, and should be considered part of the child's ongoing school program. The resource room is one of the most logical approaches to differentiation of instruction for those children who are identified as gifted and talented, but who do not require full time placement in a self contained class of gifted and talented children.

The services of a resource room are often effective in meeting individual educational needs. Administrators may view the use of a resource room for gifted and talented children as a way of providing instructional support to the child and his regular classroom teacher. A resource room should also facilitate the student's placement in a regular classroom (Hammill & Wiederholt, 1972).

The Itinerant Teacher

An itinerant teacher approach employs the skills and expertise of a teacher trained in the education of the gifted and talented. This person is responsible for serving gifted and talented students in separate schools and at various grade levels. This option provides gifted and talented students with release time from their regular classroom to pursue activities designed to challenge their unique abilities.

Since the itinerant teacher interacts with gifted and talented children on a limited basis, emphasis is placed on process rather than product. The development of higher thinking skills, creativity, and self motivation are common goals. Administrators, especially those in rural areas and/or with limited staff budgets, should give serious consideration to the use of itinerant teachers for the gifted and talented. Administrators may also consider staffing resource rooms for the gifted and talented with itinerant teachers, since the purposes and logistics of both are compatible.

EFFECTIVE APPLICATION OF DIFFERENTIATION

The use of differentiated instructional techniques is a major criteria in the effective implementation of educational programs for gifted and talented students. With the increase of interest in these students and in activities designed to deliver appropriate educational challenge, the use of differentiation is even more critical. For the most effective use of differentiation, administrators should assess their individual districts to determine an accurate profile of its gifted and talented school age population. Needs assessments undertaken to determine instructional priorities should then be analyzed and divided into component parts. Each component may then be matched with the type(s) of differentiated instructional approaches considered appropriate to meet the educational needs of identified children. Within this context, differentiation may be viewed not only as a teaching strategy, but as an administrative technique that will facilitate education.

REFERENCES

Boston, B. *Developing a community based mentorship program for the gifted and talented.* Fact sheet. Reston VA: The Council for Exceptional Children, 1978.

Cohen, S. J. Acceleration and enrichment: Drawing the base line for further study. In George, W., Cohen, S., & Stanley, J. (Eds.), *Educating the gifted: Acceleration and enrichment.* Baltimore: Johns Hopkins Univ. Press, 1979.

The Council for Exceptional Children. *Curriculum for the gifted and talented.* Fact sheet. Reston VA: The Council for Exceptional Children, 1978.

Hammill, D., & Wiederholt, J. L. *The resource room: Rationale and implementation.* Philadelphia: Buttonwood Farms, 1972.

Hirsch, S. P. *Young, gifted, and handicapped: Mainstreaming high potential handicapped students into the executive high school internships program,* 1979.

Jackson, D., & Robinson, H. *Early identification of intellectually advanced children.* Paper presented at the annual convention of the National Association for Gifted Children, San Diego, October, 1977. Available from NAGC, Hot Springs AK 71901.

Martinson, R. A. Research on the gifted and talented: Its implications for education. In *Education of the gifted and talented: Report to the Congress of the United States by the US Commissioner of Education.* Washington DC: US Government Printing Office, 1972.

National Commission on Resources for Youth. *Community based mentorships for gifted and talented. Final report.* New York: National Commission on Resources for Youth, 1977. (ERIC Document Reproduction Service No. ED 150 794.)

Renzulli, J. *A guidebook for creativity programs for the gifted and talented.* Ventura CA: Ventura County Superintendent of Schools, County Office Building, 1975.

Vassar, W. G. *Designing, developing, and implementing a program for the gifted and talented.* Unpublished manuscript, 1979.

CHAPTER 6

Screening and Identification of Gifted Students

MARY M. FRASIER

The identification of students for participation in a gifted program is based on the premise that there are some children whose unique needs are best served through educational programs that differ significantly from those offered to the general school population. In order for these students to take advantage of the offering of gifted programs, however, they must first be found. It is generally agreed that identification should occur as early as possible in their school career, should be continuous, should use multiple criteria, and should involve a variety of professionals.

INTRODUCING THE IDENTIFICATION PROCESS

Identification consists of the two processes of screening and selection. During the screening process, students in the target population are assessed and observed under as standardized conditions as possible in order to examine their qualifications for participation in the gifted program. During the selection process, determinations are made regarding which of the students observed should be placed in the gifted program.

Due process procedures should be followed throughout the entire screening and selection process. For example, testing permission forms should be on file for each student. A letter describing the nature and purpose of assessment procedures should also be sent to each parent whose child is being evaluated.

The assessment instruments and observation procedures used should be based on the type of gifted program planned and the type of student sought.

There are, however, general categories of information that are collected in any screening and identification process. Descriptions and examples of these categories of information are presented in the next section.

SCREENING STUDENTS FOR GIFTED PROGRAMS

There are three principles that should guide the screening of students before they are identified and placed in a gifted program. First, screening should allow each child in the target population an opportunity to be evaluated for participation in a gifted program. Second, screening should limit the number of children who need to be evaluated in the selection process. Finally, the data collected during screening and identification provides helpful information that should be used in the planning of appropriate educational programs for the identified gifted students.

Pre-screening Procedures

Before screening school populations for potential participants in gifted programs, a placement committee should be formed. Basically, this committee determines and monitors the screening and selection process. It also insures that no one person decides who will or will not participate in the gifted program.

Placement committee members should be knowledgeable about gifted children, knowledgeable about the various procedures that can be used to identify gifted children, and knowledgeable regarding the population groups that will be considered. While the specific number of committee members should be decided by the school system, persons to be considered include the guidance counselor, the school psychologist, classroom teachers from the age group(s) and academic area(s) in which selections will be made, and the principal. The committee should be chaired by the teacher for the gifted.

A primary task of this committee is the development of a definition of the gifted. With input obtained from the needs assessment and from discussions, this committee develops a description of the type child sought and the area(s) of talent to be fostered by the gifted program.

The committee also decides the grade(s) from which children will be selected and the number of students to be served. This committee should be aware of the ability of the school system to institute a program for the gifted that encompasses grades K-12. Where a comprehensive K-12 program is not initially possible, the committee can make plans to eventually accomplish this task.

Arrangements to serve special needs populations are determined by this committee. These special needs populations include potentially gifted students from culturally diverse groups, the handicapped, and underachievers.

Methods by which standardized test measures will be interpreted, supplemental data that needs to be collected, and the degree to which nontest methods will be used to detect gifted potential are examples of decisions that must be made.

The placement committee decides which assessment procedures will be used and the persons from whom observations of gifted potential will be sought. A complete screening process includes nominations from various sources, such as parents, teachers, peers, informed community persons, and students themselves. The submission of pupil products for evaluation might be included. Test data (achievement, group intelligence, and creativity) as well as data from biographical instruments is also evaluated.

Finally, an important task of the placement committee is to plan procedures for and disseminate information regarding the screening and identification process. Knowledge thus disseminated will be especially valuable to those who must provide information regarding potential candidates for a gifted program. In addition, it can help reduce misunderstandings regarding the nature of giftedness, the characteristics of gifted children, and the manner in which they are best selected.

When to Begin Screening

Screening and identification are best accomplished during the spring of the year. By this time, persons who must provide information are better informed regarding the performance of students and are, therefore, better able to furnish information regarding their abilities. This does not mean that screening and identification cannot happen at other times during the school year.

Components of Screening Procedures

Since the purpose of the screening procedure is to develop a pool of nominees to be considered for selection, information should be collected from a number of sources. Determination of which sources and screening devices are to be used should be based on the program focus.

If the program focuses on the academically gifted, information collected should include:

1. Achievement test data
2. Group intelligence test data
3. Creativity test data
4. Teacher judgment
5. Record of academic performance
6. Judgment of parents, peers, self

If the program focuses on the development of gifts that are primarily creative, psychosocial, or in the area of the fine and performing arts, information collected should include:

1. Test data in the specific area (e.g., creativity, art, music)
2. Teacher judgment
3. Judgment of experts using techniques such as an audition or review of a student's work
4. Judgment of parents, peers, self
5. Biographical data

Group Tests of Intelligence and Achievement

Group tests of intelligence and achievement are useful as screening devices to locate potentially gifted students. However, it is strongly recommended that these test results *not* be used for final identification.

Careful consideration should be given to the establishment of cut off scores on group tests of intelligence. Based on research findings, a recommended cut off score on a group intelligence test is 115 IQ. School systems are urged, however, to determine their own cut off score, preferably based on local performance norms.

Achievement tests selected for use should measure achievement in the area(s) that will be fostered in the program. A number of group tests of intelligence and achievement that can be used in the screening process are available. However, school systems are cautioned to consult such sources as the Buros' *Mental Measurements Yearbook* (Buros, 1978) for evaluations regarding the appropriateness of a particular test before making a final selection. Then, and only then, can a wise decision be made regarding the best test to be used with the population being assessed.

Examples of frequently used group intelligence tests are the California Test of Mental Maturity, the Goodenough-Harris Drawing Test (GHDT), The Lorge-Thorndike Intelligence Tests, and the Otis-Lennon Mental Ability Test. Commonly used group achievement tests include the California Achievement Tests, Metropolitan Achievement Tests, and Standard Achievement Tests. (See Chapter 14, Identification Instruments and Measures, for complete addresses of these and all other tests subsequently discussed throughout this chapter.)

Nominations

Nominations should be sought from a variety of sources. It is important to be sure that the respondents understand each of the items used on nomination forms, and that they have had the opportunity to observe each of the behaviors listed.

Teachers are a crucial part of the nomination process. They are in an excellent position to observe students. In addition, their involvement helps to build awareness, understanding, and support of gifted programs and gifted students. A number of teacher nomination forms containing characteristics of gifted students have already been developed. Examples include the Scale for Rating Behavior Characteristics of Superior Students (Renzulli & Hartman, 1971), and nomination forms presented in *The Identification of the Gifted and Talented* (Martinson, 1975).

Peer nominations can be a useful way to identify gifted behaviors that may not be readily noticed by teachers and other educational personnel. Parents can also provide observations concerning the out of school behaviors of children that give clues to their giftedness. Community personnel such as Boys Club leaders, Boy and Girl Scout troop leaders, and ministers can provide insights into behaviors not always observable in the school.

Students should be allowed to nominate themselves as well as provide samples of their work. Self nominations may be supplemented with information from biographical inventories and autobiographies. Biographical Inventory–Form U is one that is commonly used.

Creativity Tests

Creativity tests provide assessments of students' abilities to perform in areas that are often missed by intelligence tests. A popular example, the Torrance Tests of Creative Thinking, is described as an instrument useful in identifying giftedness that also lacks cultural bias.

Identifying the Culturally Diverse Gifted

Three guidelines should be followed when identifying potentially gifted students from culturally diverse groups. The first is to use assessment instruments that are compatible with the type of program planned and the type of student sought. For example, if an academic program is planned, procedures that identify academic performance should be used. If a program for the creatively gifted or an area in the fine and performing arts is planned, then appropriate criteria should be used to screen and select participants.

The second guideline relates to the well documented finding that students from culturally diverse backgrounds score, on the average, 15 points lower on intelligence tests than students from White Anglo-Saxon Protestant groups. This point differential has been most often attributed to lack of experiences reflected in low socioeconomic environments. A decision should be made during screening to continue processing any culturally diverse student who scores within a 15 point range below the established cut off score. This guideline is necessary to assure that students are not eliminated from consideration before additional data can be collected to substantiate their eligibility.

The third guideline relates to the use of within-group norms as well as between-group and national norms to rank abilities. For students who have not had experiences comparable to those of a more advantaged group, it is most important to compare their performance with students from similar backgrounds. A point by point comparison with students from more advantaged backgrounds may result in erroneous evaluation and exclusion of eligible culturally diverse students.

Instruments

Several instruments have been offered to assist in locating gifted students from culturally diverse backgrounds. Each has been designed to compensate for experiences and skills not normally felt to be possessed by children from culturally diverse backgrounds. These instruments should not be considered as substitutions for other tests, but as instruments that can provide supplementary data when screening and selecting students from culturally diverse backgrounds.

Tests appropriate for use with the culturally diverse gifted include the Raven's Progressive Matrices, the Torrance Tests of Creative Thinking, the Biographical Inventory–Form U, and the Leiter International Performance Scale. The Abbreviated Binet for Disadvantaged (ABDA), a form of the Stanford Binet, allows for scoring of only those Binet items that depict strengths among disadvantaged Blacks.

The IPAT Culture Fair Intelligence Tests (Scales I, II, and III) are useful with persons having different national languages and cultures or those influenced by very different social status and education. The System of Multicultural Pluralistic Assessment is designed to assess students according to norms established within the cultural group. The California Environmental Based Screen is designed to identify mentally gifted students whose limited exposure outside the radius of their community minimizes their perception and range of responses. It allows a second look at a child, and the results obtained are useful in confirming or rejecting a child as exceptional. The Structure of Intellect (SOI) Test of Learning Abilities is a diagnostic procedure for testing patterns of strengths in disadvantaged Black, Chicano, American Indian, and Anglo students.

Rating Scales and Procedures

The Los Angeles Unified School District has developed a scale for detecting gifted children from culturally diverse backgrounds that includes behavioral traits as well as a checklist for describing various kinds of deprivations (economic, language, etc.). It is available in *The Identification of the Gifted and Talented* (Martinson, 1975). Joyce Gay has developed a procedure for identifying academically gifted Black students (Gay, 1978). Included in the procedure is a comparative characteristics checklist of gifted indicators along with a process for observing leadership behaviors.

Summary

A variety of instruments and procedures have been discussed that may be used during the screening process. Used in a combination dictated by the type of student sought and the type of program planned, the chances of overlooking students who should be considered for gifted programs are greatly reduced. Decisions may be made to continue or discontinue a student in the screening process as results become available from other sources. From the pool of students remaining, selections for the program are made.

CASE STUDY AND SELECTION

During this phase, information is collected that allows the placement committee to make its final decision. Individual tests are administered and the case study is completed.

Individual Tests

Ideally, every child considered for placement in a program for the intellectually gifted should be administered an individual test. Problems such as cost and the availability of trained personnel may, however, prove to be prohibitive. Where priorities must be set, special consideration should be given to those students for whom there is discrepant data (e.g., suspected underachievers or students who may have a learning disability). Children from culturally diverse/disadvantaged backgrounds should also be considered for individual testing. Individual intelligence tests frequently used are the Stanford-Binet Intelligence Scale and the Wechsler Intelligence Scale for Children–Revised (WISC–R).

The Case Study

The case study should include all of the data needed by the placement committee to make decisions regarding which students will be admitted to the gifted program. Therefore, information such as developmental background data, psychometric and academic data, data from nomination forms, data from student self inventory, and data regarding accomplishments should all be available for consideration. Sources for case study forms include Clark (1979) and Martinson (1975).

PLACEMENT IN GIFTED PROGRAM

All information collected should now be reviewed by the placement committee. The task is to decide which students best qualify for placement in the program. Placement should be guided by the decisions made during the pre-screening phase and should be followed by a program designed to accommodate the needs of students identified. During this stage, placement committees may also consider conducting individual interviews to query students regarding their desire to participate in the gifted program.

Systems for Collecting Data

Placement committees may wish to design their own system for data collection. There are, however, several existing systems. Project Improve (Renzulli, 1978) offers a system that provides a plan for collecting data in both the screening and the selection process. A form is included for collecting and processing data at each step in the system. The Baldwin Identification Matrix (see Chapter 14) is a system for deciding, recording, and weighing data to be used in identifying students for gifted programs.

REFERENCES

Buros, O. K. (Ed.). *The eighth mental measurements yearbook.* Highland Park NJ: Gryphon, 1978.

Clark, B. *Growing up gifted: Developing the potential of children at home and at school.* Columbus OH: Charles E. Merrill, 1979.

Gay, J. E. Proposed plan for identifying black gifted children. *Gifted Child Quarterly*, 1978, *22* (3), 353–360.

Martinson, R. A. *The identification of the gifted and talented.* Reston VA: The Council for Exceptional Children, 1975.

Renzulli, J. S. *Project Improve: Report of the task force on identification.* Hartford: Connecticut State Department of Education, 1978.

Renzulli, J. S., & Hartman, R. K. Scale for rating behavioral characteristics of superior students. *Exceptional Children*, 1971, *38* (3), 243–248.

CHAPTER 7

Programing for the Culturally Diverse

MARY M. FRASIER

Who are the culturally diverse gifted? What are they like? What factors are important when designing gifted programs in which they participate? What factors should be considered when implementing gifted programs in which they participate? Answers to these questions will guide this discussion.

WHO ARE THESE CHILDREN AND WHAT ARE THEY LIKE?

In this discussion, the term *culturally diverse* gifted is used to refer to those children who come from Black, Mexican American, Puerto Rican, and American Indian populations. Of the numerous terms that have been applied to them, culturally diverse is felt to be more appropriate because it emphasizes the diversity within their cultural groups without implying any value judgment regarding the nature of these variations.

Culturally diverse children are often mistakenly viewed as a monolithic whole. The wide spectrum of variability within cultural groups is frequently disregarded. However, as within any cultural group, culturally diverse children vary along many dimensions.

Socioeconomic Dimension

Disadvantaged is the term used to refer to children from low socioeconomic backgrounds. While a large proportion of culturally diverse children are disadvantaged, not all of them are.

By comparison, the educational preparation, home environment, and value systems of gifted culturally diverse children from advantaged backgrounds are very much like those of advantaged children from other cultural groups. Discrimination because of race, ethnic group, or regional subcultural group membership is the major disadvantage they may encounter.

Culturally diverse gifted children who are also disadvantaged face other problems besides discrimination. First, research on disadvantaged children has tended to concentrate on their academic difficulties. Such characteristics as underdeveloped abstract thinking abilities, language deficiency, poor reading skills, short attention span, and inefficient test taking skills frequently appear in the literature as descriptors of disadvantaged children. All children from disadvantaged backgrounds are assumed to possess these same characteristics and to the same degree. As a result, the assumption has prevailed that gifted and talented culturally diverse children, especially in the intellectual category, cannot be found.

On the opposite side, an equally critical problem is encountered. When culturally diverse gifted children from disadvantaged backgrounds are identified, program practices for them tend to resemble the remedial and compensatory efforts developed for their nongifted peers.

Psychosocial Dimension

Anti-intellectual attitudes, external locus of control, inability to delay gratification, low motivation (especially for academic pursuits), and negative self image are typical of the traits appearing in the literature to describe culturally diverse children. This deficit approach to describing these children is often used whether they are gifted or not. Such unilateral comparisons contribute to the continuation of the unsubstantiated opinion that culturally diverse gifted students, especially the disadvantaged, bring these kinds of learner characteristics to gifted programs.

Quite the opposite is true. Shade (1978) summarized data from studies on high achievers from a culturally diverse group, reporting that they were goal oriented, possessed great self confidence, and felt positive about themselves. Data indicated that they tended to feel that they were in control of their destiny, had high levels of aspiration, and possessed confidence that they would accomplish their goals. These achievers were also characterized as demonstrating a need to be cautious, controlled, less trusting, and constricting in their approach to their environment. They were further described as highly original and creative in their ideas and exhibited a tendency to be shrewd and manipulative of the situations in which they found themselves.

Davidson and Greenberg (1967) examined personality variables that differentiated between high and low achievers from lower class backgrounds. Traits found to differentiate between these two groups were similar to those found to distinguish between middle class achievers and underachievers. These traits included ego strength, well developed controls and self confidence, greater maturity and seriousness of interest, the need to seek adult approval, and a willingness to postpone immediate pleasures.

It is often overlooked that there are many well adjusted, well cared for children growing up in inner city environments who are reinforced in intellectual pursuits. The realization of this state of affairs has serious import for the design and implementation of programs for these children.

Environmental Dimension

What is the nature of the home environments of culturally diverse populations that produce achievers? Quite often the low academic performance of culturally diverse children is attributed to the lack of ability of lower class homes to provide relevant experiences with academic materials, activities, and language. These conditions, generally resulting from poverty, obscure the true nature of many homes of disadvantaged children, especially those who are achievers.

The home environments of culturally diverse children from advantaged backgrounds is very much like that of children from other cultural groups who achieve. The parents are well educated, have high educational aspirations for their children, and provide them with numerous educational opportunities and experiences.

While adverse conditions of life do not facilitate academic achievement, there is no evidence that such conditions preclude academic success (Gordon & Wilkerson, 1966). For low socioeconomic parents, providing conditions that facilitate the development of intellectual ability is more difficult, but it is not impossible. Despite the existence of handicapping social and economic conditions, there are many parents of disadvantaged children who place a high value on education. This characteristic immediately dispels the generalization that culturally diverse children come from homes that are anti-intellectual.

Coleman (1969) explored the nature of disadvantaged homes that produce successful achievers. It was revealed that there was strong parental encouragement for the children to do well in school, to read, to have hobbies, and to make friends. Praise was frequently used as a reward for accomplishments. Parents were interested and involved in their children's lives and required them to meet certain obligations such as doing homework and exhibiting approved standards of behavior. A helpful and stimulating atmosphere existed in the home and a feeling of mutual respect existed between parent and child.

Prototypes

Factors to be discussed which affect the designing and implementation of programs for the culturally diverse gifted are based on one of the following prototypes.

Student A

This culturally diverse gifted student comes from a middle class home where the parents are well educated and hold high educational aspirations for their children. Students of this type have attended good schools where they were superior academic performers. They are mature, well adjusted, and goal oriented. They also have confidence that they can accomplish their goals.

Student B

This student comes from a lower class but well organized home. Despite socioeconomic handicaps, the parents hold high aspirations for their children to achieve academically and occupationally. Parents are active encouragers and reinforcers of educational pursuits. Sacrifices are made in order that their children may have certain educational opportunities. Students of this type have high aspirations, and are usually confident that they can achieve their goals.

Student C

This student comes from a working class home. The parents express a desire for their children to obtain an education though they may lack the skills to assist them. Achievers from this type of environment are usually well cared for and have a positive self image. They are confident that they can achieve, although their aspirations may be somewhat narrow.

Student D

This student comes from the kind of lower class home typically described in research literature. The parents have little education; the father is usually absent; the mother usually works at a low level job; and there are often a large number of siblings. There is a limited educational tradition in the home, and the day to day preoccupation with survival tends to divert attention away from planning for the future.

Implications

Culturally diverse gifted students like Student A should have very little difficulty fitting into traditional programs for the gifted. Their abilities and experiences will be very much like those of other high achievers who come from similar backgrounds, regardless of race or ethnic group.

The motivation to excel is a typical characteristic of Students B and C. The achievement of both is above average, with Student B possibly achieving at levels closer to Student A. Both of these students may face problems if teachers base expectations for their performance on assumptions they make about low socioeconomic environment. It is most important that they be given opportunities to demonstrate their true abilities to perform.

The attitude of Student C will be an important factor to consider when implementing gifted programs. The level of motivation exhibited by students of this type will depend upon the degree to which the educational environment is perceived to be responsive to their efforts to perform according to their capabilities.

Students of the type described as Student D present the greatest challenge. Greater efforts will have to be expended to provide new and broader experiences for them. Many opportunities will need to be provided through which their ability to achieve is encouraged and supported.

Given this perspective of the various types of gifted culturally diverse students, what factors are important to consider when designing programs for them? As stated earlier, Student A should fit very easily into traditionally planned gifted programs. Therefore, the remainder of this discussion focuses on factors particularly pertinent to Students B, C, and D.

Basic factors. The first factor that must be considered and accepted is that these students are indeed gifted. Adverse conditions of their environment should be taken into consideration, but must not be viewed as precluding their ability to succeed. The demonstrated success of many individuals from adverse backgrounds makes this an untenable position.

Secondly, programs for these students should be designed to meet needs that *cannot* be met or are not being met in a curriculum designed for the average student. Third, program experiences for these students should be based on data obtained during screening and selection rather than on preconceived notions regarding ability to perform. Martinson (1975, p. 108) pointed out that "the tendency to apply group sociological findings and to think in group terms rather than to center on the individual has caused much of the indifference to giftedness among the disadvantaged." Teacher expectations should be based on accurate and sensitive data gathered on the individual.

Finally, programs for these students should provide opportunities for them to explore in depth the areas in which they are interested. This is a fundamental premise underlying programs for the gifted.

Mental traits. Though these children differ in many respects, they do hold certain mental traits in common. These have been defined as:

1. The ability to meaningfully manipulate some symbol system.
2. The ability to think logically, given appropriate data.
3. The ability to use stored knowledge to solve problems.
4. The ability to reason by analogy.
5. The ability to extend or extrapolate knowledge to new situations or unique applications. (Gallagher & Kinney, 1974)

Needs. In one sense, the needs of these gifted culturally diverse children are similar to those of other gifted children. Minority group membership, however, adds another dimension to these needs. According to Frasier (1979),

> They face similar issues and must resolve similar conflicts as they attempt to make appropriate educational and vocational decisions, deal with pressures from parents, peers, and others because of their giftedness, and deal with their more rapid advancement through various developmental stages. However, for the diverse gifted these needs are intensified because, more often than not, they are members of minority groups. In addition, their perspective of their ability, based on varied reactions from theirs and other cultures, adds another dimension to their problem that is not present in the lives of other gifted children. Thus, their sense of need is heightened as they attempt to cope with the many problems associated with their above average ability. (p. 304)

Summary

The intent of this discussion has not been to dismiss the realities of growing up in a poor environment nor the problems associated with minority group membership. Rather, the intent was to caution against overgeneralizations and the drawing of too many cause–effect conclusions without substantiating evidence.

There are gifted children in culturally diverse groups. They come from both advantaged and disadvantaged backgrounds. This finding is no less true of other cultural groups outside the focus of this discussion. Gifted culturally diverse children are more like their gifted peers from other cultural groups than they are like their nongifted culturally diverse peers. The following discussion delineates specific factors and offers specific suggestions relative to program design and implementation for these children.

PROGRAM FACTORS

When designing and implementing programs for gifted and talented children from culturally diverse backgrounds, program planners should emphasize their giftedness rather than their disadvantages. Preoccupation with the problems and difficulties of the culturally diverse gifted who are disadvantaged, rather than an emphasis on their potential to achieve, causes attention to be directed toward remedial experiences that these children are judged to need in order to "catch up" or compensatory experiences needed in order to "make up." Programs for gifted culturally diverse children must instead be built on those assets, behaviors, and conditions which can be used to aid them in performing according to their predicted potential.

Administrative Support

When designing programs for the culturally diverse gifted, administrative support is necessary. The design and development of programs require close cooperation and support from the administration. The type and quality of programs developed will depend heavily on the attitude conveyed at the administrative level. Administrators should communicate two very important concepts: (1) that gifted and talented students can be found in culturally diverse populations; and (2) that these students can be simultaneously different *and* excellent.

To communicate these ideas, administrators need to create an atmosphere of awareness in the school regarding gifted children from culturally diverse backgrounds. They should interpret to staff, students, parents, and the community a position that reflects the school's goal to find and develop the potential that exists in these populations.

It is, first of all, imperative that administrators accept the fact that children from culturally diverse backgrounds are capable of above average achievement in academic, creative, leadership, and fine and performing arts areas. Secondly, it is imperative that administrators establish and foster an atmosphere of striving for excellence among teachers, students, and parents. Within the school, inservice programs to acquaint the total staff with the characteristics and unique needs of culturally diverse gifted students are desirable and needed.

Administrators should plan and make available mechanisms to allow and encourage input from a variety of sources when designing programs to accommodate the needs of culturally diverse gifted students. These sources include parents, students, and community organizations personnel. Relationships with community resources that can support program development for these students should also be developed.

Multiple Program Prototypes

Multiple program prototypes should be available to meet the educational needs of the culturally diverse gifted. Many different types of intra and extra classroom prototypes should be used in order to provide culturally diverse gifted children with numerous learning opportunities. It is very important that they be exposed to experiences they may have missed due to social and economic limitations.

Examples of program prototypes include back to back classes or block scheduling; field trips; mentorship programs; independent study; cluster grouping in special classes for the gifted and in the regular classroom; ungraded classes; minicourses; and interest clubs. Guidelines for the selection of these and other prototypes should be based on the ability of the prototype to provide expanded learning opportunities where groups or individuals may develop, explore, and experience new learning possibilities, interact with and be reinforced by peers of similar ability, and benefit from contact with tutors and mentors.

Opportunities for Stimulation

Programs for the culturally diverse gifted must provide opportunities for educational and occupational stimulation. Schools that have been successful with the culturally diverse high achiever, according to Sowell (1972), inspired their students with the confidence that they could do anything in spite of anything. They emphasized abstract subjects and used no discernibly different teaching strategies such as those typically suggested for use with disadvantaged students.

"They gave me really good advice. They withheld opinions as far as go here, go there. But they gave me a lot of help in weighing different places and made me make the decision for myself." This statement was made by a student enrolled in a program that successfully assisted high achieving inner city youth to enter medical careers (Shepherd, 1972).

A study by Glaser and Ross (1970) listed 14 characteristics that described achievers from seriously disadvantaged backgrounds. Examples of those that are relevant to this discussion were a questioning orientation; being aware of alternative paths; identification with supportive role models and supportive and inspiring relationships; and a risk taking capacity. These traits were not developed without assistance in both formal and informal situations. They are useful to consider when determining appropriate program experiences for the culturally diverse gifted.

Program implementation should stress the four areas of objectives proposed by Taba and Elkins (1966). They are (1) knowledge or acquisition of facts; (2) thinking or ways of reflecting on these facts; (3) attitudes or the development of experiences and materials that impact on individual feelings; and (4) skills which are developed primarily through practice, preferably in different contexts. In addition, the following program features are critical.

Interaction

Opportunities to interact with significant others may be offered with mentors or through literature. As stated by Taba and Elkins (1966), "literature . . . can be used for sensitivity training, as a means of extending limited experiences with human behavior and the problems of human relations." While mentor relationships are very important for the prototypes described as Students B and C, they are critical for Student D.

Awareness of Alternatives

Although many of these students have the ability to achieve, they are often unaware of the alternative paths and opportunities available to them. Programs for the culturally diverse gifted should provide numerous opportunities through simulations, role playing, imagery techniques, and the like in which alternative futures can be explored.

Development of Inquiry Skills

Learning how to inquire is a critical skill that requires development. These students, especially C and D, need opportunities to learn how to separate relevant from irrelevant information. In addition, learning about different resources that can be consulted for information is important. Experiences in decision making, inquiry training, and learning how to ask questions are all helpful in developing inquiry skills.

Summary

Many of the factors to be considered when planning programs for the culturally diverse gifted are the same as those for other gifted children. The degree of attention that must be paid to some of these factors, however, may differ. For example, program planners are reminded of the importance of considering the characteristics and needs of the individual. Attention to needs that cannot be met or are not being met in the regular classroom is also very important.

The programs that can be developed to nurture the potential of children from culturally diverse backgrounds are limited only by our imagination. The rewards from accepting and meeting the challenge, however, far exceed our imagination.

REFERENCES

Coleman, A. B. The disadvantaged child who is successful in school. *The Education Forum*, November 1969, 95–97.

Davidson, H. H., & Greenberg, J. W. *Traits of school achievers from a deprived background*. New York: The City College of the City University of New York, 1967. (Project No. 2805. Contract No. OE-5-10-132)

Frasier, M. M. Counseling the culturally diverse gifted. In N. Colangelo & R. T. Zaffrann (Eds.), *New voices in counseling the gifted*. Dubuque IA: Kendall/Hunt, 1979.

Gallagher, J., & Kinney, L. *Talent delayed–talent denied: The culturally different gifted child: A conference report*. Reston VA: The Council for Exceptional Children, 1974.

Glaser, E. M., & Ross, H. L. A *study of successful persons from seriously disadvantaged backgrounds: Final report*. Washington DC: Department of Labor, Office of Special Manpower Programs, 1970. (Contract No. 82-05-68-03)

Gordon, E. W., & Wilkerson, D. A. *Compensatory education for the disadvantaged. Programs and practices: Pre-school through college.* New York: College Entrance Board, 1966.

Martinson, R. A. *The identification of the gifted and talented.* Reston VA: The Council for Exceptional Children, 1975.

Shade, B. J. Social-psychological traits of achieving black children. *The Negro Educational Review*, 1978, *29*, 80–86.

Shepherd, J. Black lab power. *Saturday Review*, 1972, 33–39.

Sowell, T. *Black education: Myths and tragedies.* New York: David McKay, 1972.

Taba, H., & Elkins, D. *Teaching strategies for the culturally disadvantaged.* Chicago: Rand McNally, 1966.

CHAPTER 8

Designing and Operating Programs for the Gifted and Talented Handicapped

EDWINA D. PENDARVIS and JOHN A. GROSSI

Having successfully overcome false notions that gifted children are puny, bespectacled introverts, advocates of the gifted today face the important challenge of combatting yet another stereotype. Terman's studies (Terman & Oden, 1947) and others which followed have resulted in an image of the gifted child as physically superior, socially adept, and highly motivated to achieve (Maker, 1977). While this image may be more representative of the group as a whole, there are many gifted children who do not fit the mold: gifted children from economically disadvantaged homes, gifted children from cultures which do not subscribe to middle class values, and gifted children whose poor performance may stem from adjustment or attitudinal problems. These children are in danger of being overlooked even in this era of rapid growth in gifted programs.

CONCERN FOR THE GIFTED HANDICAPPED

Recently, there has been growing concern for another group of children who do not fit the Terman image of the gifted child as superior in physical, emotional, and social development. This newly recognized group is the gifted handicapped.

Concern for gifted handicapped children is warranted for several reasons. The most obvious is that a child with a handicap is not likely to be recognized as gifted. It is understandable that teachers may have difficulty in recognizing giftedness in a bright fifth grader who cannot read because of a specific learning disability. Emotional problems, sensory deficits, learning disabilities, and health problems effectively mask superior potential in many children.

A second cause for concern is that the combination of giftedness and a handicapping condition creates unique problems for the child, the parents, and the school system. Understanding and dealing with these problems requires extensive communication and coordination between gifted educators, school administrators, educators of handicapped children, counselors, regular classroom teachers, and parents.

Yet another source of concern is that gifted children who have mild or moderate handicaps may not receive needed intervention because their intellectual ability enables them to compensate enough to perform on their grade level. Intervention is often limited to children who are making poor grades or disrupting the class. The child who is doing average work, but who is capable of doing much better, is seldom referred for special education services.

DEFINITION OF THE GIFTED HANDICAPPED POPULATION

Gifted handicapped children may be defined as those who come under the definition of giftedness established in the Gifted and Talented Children's Education Act of 1978 and who also meet the definition of the handicapped set forth in Public Law 94-142, the Education for All Handicapped Children Act. According to the federal definition, children may be eligible for gifted programs on the basis of superior intellectual ability, specific academic ability, creativity, leadership, or ability in the visual or performing arts. Programs for the handicapped are provided for children who are identified as mentally retarded, hard of hearing, deaf, speech impaired, visually handicapped, seriously emotionally disturbed, orthopedically or other health impaired, deaf-blind, multihandicapped, or learning disabled.

The multitude of possible combinations of giftedness and handicaps is obvious. Superior ability of every kind has been found among the various categories of handicapping conditions. Helen Keller, Franklin Roosevelt, Sarah Bernhardt, Winston Churchill, George Shearing, Thomas Edison, Ben Hogan, Ludwig Von Beethoven, and Elizabeth Barrett Browning are only a few of many eminent handicapped intellectuals, artists, and athletes.

We do not know the incidence of giftedness among the handicapped population, but there may be many more gifted handicapped children than previously thought. As methods of educational and psychological evaluation become more sophisticated, we should discover unsuspected strengths in handicapped children. We will probably also find that some "average" students are gifted children with learning or emotional handicaps.

Defining "gifted handicapped" is a relatively easy task compared to the difficult and complex problem of identifying gifted handicapped children and providing the educational and support services they need. Despite the difficulty, more and more schools are combining the skills and resources of educators of the gifted, educators of the handicapped, classroom teachers, administrators, and counselors to discover solutions. The purpose of this chapter is to discuss major obstacles to education for the gifted handicapped and to suggest methods which have shown promise for overcoming these obstacles.

EDUCATIONAL POLICY FOR THE EDUCATION OF GIFTED HANDICAPPED CHILDREN

Few education agencies have recognized the need to establish policy regarding the identification and instruction of gifted handicapped children. Virtually all state and local education agencies have adopted policy regarding handicapped children and most have adopted policy for educating gifted children. However, there is still a need for policy statements specific to the gifted handicapped because their education presents special problems which are not adequately resolved by addressing either the handicapped population or the gifted population separately.

The fact that concern for the gifted handicapped is relatively new requires that attention be drawn to this group. Formal commitment to their education should be made in order to assure development of suitable programs. Such commitment should be part of a state plan for gifted and talented children. According to Grossi (1980), the development and implementation of an operational state plan for the gifted and talented, including the gifted handicapped, is a major factor in assuring the provision of appropriate educational programs and services. State plans are essential organizational guidelines that provide direction and facilitation to state and local personnel in the delivery of educational services. Like public policy, a state plan reflects the concerns of the environment and situation in which it was developed.

Policy statements regarding the gifted handicapped should acknowledge that there is evidence that many handicapped children are unidentified gifted children; that there are gifted children with unrecognized handicaps; and that consequently, many children who belong to both groups are inadequately served. Commitment to improve services to these children can be operationalized by policy statements addressing awareness, identification, educational planning, and instruction. The sample policy statement on the following page may serve as a model.

SAMPLE POLICY STATEMENT:
THE EDUCATION OF GIFTED HANDICAPPED CHILDREN

According to Public Law 94-142, the Education for All Handicapped Children Act, a free appropriate public education must be available to all handicapped children aged 3 to 21. It is the belief of this agency that gifted handicapped children have unique educational needs and that failure to identify and address those needs constitutes neglect of professional responsibilities.

In order to assure the availability of a free appropriate public education to handicapped children who are also gifted, the following efforts will be undertaken:

- All administrative personnel will be charged with the responsibility of making instructional, supervisory, and support personnel aware of the need for special attention to the needs of gifted handicapped children.
- Screening methods used for the identification of handicapped children will include measures designed to determine the special strengths and interests of handicapped children.
- Assessment of handicapped children will include measures which will evaluate the strengths indicated through screening.
- Individualized education plans for handicapped children who are gifted will include objectives which address the strengths of the child as well as the weaknesses.
- A person qualified to teach gifted children will serve on the committee responsible for the development of an individualized education plan for a child who is both handicapped and gifted.
- A handicapped child who is gifted will be placed in a program for gifted children unless there is evidence that the child will not benefit from such placement.
- A teacher qualified to teach gifted children will provide support and assistance to regular classroom or special education teachers who are responsible for the education of gifted handicapped children.

In addition to the efforts listed above, this agency will realize its commitment to gifted handicapped children by establishing a systematic means of involving parents in the education of gifted handicapped children; identifying human, fiscal, and informational resources which will facilitate the education of gifted handicapped children; and creating public awareness of the contributions which gifted handicapped children can make to society and of their right to the educational services which maximize their own self fulfillment.

METHODS FOR SCREENING, IDENTIFICATION, AND EDUCATIONAL ASSESSMENT

Although guidelines for screening, identification, and educational assessment of gifted handicapped children should be included in the state plan, the task of evaluating the potential of gifted handicapped children generally falls to the local school district. At this level, the major obstacle to appropriate educational services is a lack of understanding of this group of children. Inservice training for school personnel and for parents is essential to discovering talent among the handicapped and handicaps among the talented. Training should range from awareness campaigns to intensive, skill building sessions for educational diagnosticians and other involved professionals. The following procedures include suggestions for addressing this obstacle to finding, placing, and designing educational plans for gifted handicapped children.

Screening

The first step in educational planning for the gifted handicapped is screening. Suggested procedures for screening are based on practices which have been used in federally funded projects for gifted handicapped children and may be modified to suit local practices and resources.

Awareness Sessions

Prior to collection of referrals, awareness sessions for regular classroom teachers, teachers of handicapped children, teachers of gifted children, and parents should be conducted. Topics for discussion include:

- Importance of special attention to the needs of gifted handicapped children.
- Characteristics of gifted children.
- Ways in which various handicapping conditions can mask superior abilities.
- Importance of recognizing and developing the strengths of all handicapped children.
- Distribution and explanation of behavior checklists/rating scales to be used to evaluate the children.

Observations

Participants in the awareness sessions should use what they have learned to observe their children and decide whether referral for special services is indicated.

Data and Relevant Information

In their referrals, teachers and parents should provide behavioral checklists, anecdotal information illustrating unusual ability, and evidence of outstanding performance such as awards or prizes. Teachers should provide standardized test scores from cumulative records, although the committee receiving referrals must interpret these in the light of possible effects of handicapping conditions.

Identification

Identification, as used here, refers to procedures used to determine whether a child meets eligibility criteria which have been established to distinguish those children who are most likely to benefit from special services. In most local school districts, a multidisciplinary committee has the responsibility for receiving referrals and determining, on the basis of screening information, what types of further evaluation are needed to determine whether the referred child needs special education.

Standardized Tests

An important obstacle in this process for the gifted handicapped child is in the use of standardized test instruments typically employed for determining eligibility for services. Identification of gifted children usually includes consideration of performance on standardized tests. However, we can make inferences based on such tests only under certain conditions. According to Mercer and Lewis (1978), children whose performance is being compared with a norm must:

1. Have had similar opportunities to learn the materials and acquire the skills covered in the test.
2. Have been similarly motivated by the significant other persons in their lives to learn this material and acquire these skills.
3. Have had similar experience with taking tests.
4. Have no emotional disturbances or anxieties interfering with test performance.
5. Have no sensorimotor disabilities interfering with prior learning or with their ability to respond in the test situation. (p. 9)

It is apparent that these conditions are not in effect when we compare the performance of handicapped children with that of nonhandicapped children. In order to make inferences about the learning potential of the handicapped, we must find ways to satisfy these conditions. One way is to use tests which have been standardized on a population with a handicapping condition similar to that of the child being tested. For example, the Leiter

TABLE 1

Popular Instruments Used in the Identification of Gifted Handicapped Children

Handicapping Condition[a]	Intellectual Ability	Specific Academic Ability	Creativity	Leadership	Ability in the Visual or Performing Arts
MR	Stanford-Binet Intelligence Scale or Wechsler Intelligence Scale for Children-Revised (WISC-R)	Differential Aptitude Tests (DAT) Peabody Individual Achievement Test (PIAT) SOI Learning Abilities Test	Torrance Tests of Creative Thinking (administered individually)	Sociograms and/or behavior checklists completed by peers and teachers	Samples of performance judged by experts
LD	Performance or Verbal scale of Wechsler Intelligence Scale for Children-Revised	DAT PIAT Scholastic Aptitude Test (SAT) SOI Learning Abilities Test	Torrance Tests of Creative Thinking (administered individually) Alpha Biographical Inventory	Sociograms/ behavior checklists	Samples of performance judged by experts

SI	Leiter International Performance Scale	DAT	Torrance Tests of Creative Thinking (administered individually)	Sociograms/ behavior checklists	Samples of performance judged by experts
		PIAT			
	Boehm Test of Basic Concepts (preschool/ kindergarten)	SAT	Alpha Biographical Inventory		
		SOI Learning Abilities Test			
	Peabody Picture Vocabulary Test (if child has difficulty responding orally)				
HI	Leiter International Performance Scale	DAT	Torrance Tests of Creative Thinking (given by interpreter for deaf if child can't read)	Sociograms/ behavior checklists	Samples of performance judged by experts
		PIAT			
		SAT			
		SOI Learning Abilities Test (administered by interpreter if child can't read)			

TABLE 1 (continued)

Handicapping Condition [a]	Intellectual Ability	Specific Academic Ability	Creativity	Leadership	Ability in the Visual or Performing Arts
VI	Interim Hayes Binet Intelligence Test for the Blind	DAT PIAT SAT SOI Learning Abilities Test (given orally)	Torrance Tests of Creative Thinking (verbal form, given orally)	Sociograms/behavior checklists	Samples of performance judged by experts
PH	Stanford-Binet or WISC-R, modified so that less motor control is needed to respond	Tests of specific aptitude given orally or modified	Torrance Tests of Creative Thinking (modified so that less motor control is required)	Sociograms/behavior checklists	Samples of performance judged by experts

[a] MR mentally retarded
LD learning disabled
SI speech impaired
HI hearing impaired
VI visually impaired
PH physically handicapped

International Performance Scale, a nonverbal intelligence test, has norms for hearing impaired children.

Another way is to locate tests which are not likely to cause the handicapping condition to interfere with performance. Most IQ tests demand considerable skill with language. Children who have hearing impairments, speech problems, or disabilities in processing language may have extraordinary intellectual ability which will not show up on such tests. Again, the Leiter or another nonverbal test should give a much more accurate picture of intellectual development. Children who understand language but cannot produce it can be given the Peabody Picture Vocabulary Test.

An approach which has shown much promise is that of trial programing, giving children opportunities to practice tasks similar to those on the test. Many handicapped children have been segregated from the regular classroom and lack experience with the types of problems encountered on standardized tests. Providing that experience improves the accuracy of measurement of their potential.

Still another approach is to modify tests so that physical or sensory deficits do not interfere with performance. This method has been used to measure creative ability among physically handicapped children by enlarging the stimulus items and response space on the Torrance Tests of Creative Thinking so that less motor control is required (White, 1976). Table 1 indicates instruments popularly used in the identification of gifted handicapped children along dimensions of ability areas and handicapping conditions.

Training for diagnosticians should include all of the approaches suggested above. A multifaceted or case study approach to identification is essential. Educational diagnosticians must be able to use a variety of evaluative techniques, both formal and informal. Inservice must enable the personnel responsible for evaluation to select, modify, and interpret evaluative measures in light of particular combinations of ability and handicap (e.g., creativity in blind children). Interpretation of evaluation results requires the combined expertise of educators of the gifted and educators of handicapped children, as well as that of diagnostic personnel.

Steps in the Identification Process

The identification process includes the following steps:

1. The placement committee reviews information collected through the screening process and makes a tentative determination of handicapping condition, possible talent areas, and types of further evaluation needed.
2. The diagnostician and other professional personnel select and administer appropriate evaluative measures.
3. The committee reviews and interprets the results of the evaluation.

4. A decision is made by the committee as to whether special services are needed. (If results are questionable, further evaluation may be recommended.)
5. For children determined to need special services, the committee recommends assessment procedures which will aid in the development of an individualized education program (IEP).

Assessment for IEP Development

Each child who is identified as gifted based on the preceding levels of evaluation should be provided an indepth educational assessment which can be used in development of an individualized education program for the child. At this point, information as to specific educational levels, special interests, and preferred styles of learning is important (Renzulli & Smith, 1979). Table 2 presents major elements of screening, identification, and assessment of gifted handicapped children.

The child's performance level in various subject areas can be determined using informal teacher-made tests and/or commercial skill inventories such as IBAS (Instruction-Based Appraisal System) or BCP (Behavioral Characteristics Progression). Many school districts have sequenced their curricula into objectives which can easily be converted into test questions. A summary of the child's performance levels can be made on the basis of the educational assessment.

Since most gifted programs base instruction on student interests as well as ability, an inventory of special interests should be conducted. This, too, can be either teacher-made or commercial. Renzulli (1977) has designed an interest questionnaire for gifted children which could be adapted as needed for the gifted handicapped.

Many handicapped children have difficulty learning through particular sensory modalities. For example, visually impaired children and many learning disabled children have difficulty taking in information visually. Instruction using tactile or auditory approaches will be more effective. Teachers of handicapped children can suggest methods for discovering which sensory channel each child uses most efficiently. Renzulli and Smith (1979) suggested that educators find out the type(s) of instruction preferred by gifted children and select teaching strategies accordingly. They have developed a learning styles questionnaire for that purpose.

The involvement of parents is important in developing the IEP for a gifted handicapped child, just as it is in screening and evaluation for identification. They know the child better than anyone, and can offer valuable input to evaluation and planning. Parents should be included in each of the following steps of IEP development.

1. The committee reviews information collected during the screening and identification processes. This information is particularly helpful in suggesting appropriate educational placement and major educational goals.
2. Involved instructional personnel administer formal and informal educational mastery tests, interest inventories, and learning style inventories.
3. The committee reviews the results; recommends educational objectives, strategies, and materials; and determines the educational setting(s) which should be most beneficial.

INSTRUCTIONAL PROGRAMS FOR GIFTED HANDICAPPED CHILDREN

Educational Placement

Should gifted handicapped children be educated with gifted children, with handicapped children, or in the regular classroom? In many cases, the answer is "yes" to all three placements. Children with severe handicaps usually require at least part time placement with similarly handicapped children to receive intensive educational services provided by the special education teacher. However, these children still need the stimulation of gifted children and the opportunity for social interaction with children in the regular classroom as well. Children with mild handicaps may be best served by dual placement in a gifted program and the regular classroom with support and assistance provided by the special education teacher.

The best placement for each child can be decided by reviewing the goals and objectives of the IEP and deciding in which setting(s) they are most likely to be accomplished. For example, remediation of mathematical weaknesses may be carried out in the regular classroom. Special instruction, such as mobility training for the visually impaired or communication skills for children with language difficulties, may be most readily provided in a special education resource room. Development of creative problem solving skills may be carried out in a small group setting with other gifted children.

Many gifted handicapped children could benefit from working with handicapped adults with similar interests who could serve as role models. This could be accomplished on campus or, for older students, in the community. Whatever the placement, communication and cooperation among the child's teachers are essential to achieving a balance between enhancing strengths and remediating weaknesses. The sample IEP at the end of this chapter illustrates the use of special educational settings for gifted handicapped children, using the example of a learning disabled gifted child.

Instruction for Affective Development

Interviews with gifted handicapped adults reveal that the emotional adjustment of this group is an important instructional consideration (Leonard,

TABLE 2

Major Elements of Screening, Identification, and Assessment of Gifted Handicapped Children

Evaluation Level	Evaluation Procedures	Personnel Involved	Use of Results
Screening	Completion of behavior checklists/rating scales	Regular classroom teachers	Establishment of pool of names of handicapped children who may be gifted
	Collection of available standardized test scores	Teachers of handicapped children	
		Parents	
	Collection of information on outstanding achievement	Peers	
Identification	Review of screening information	Administrator	Determination of handicapped children eligible for gifted program
	Administration of standardized and/or nonstandardized tests	Diagnostician	
		Regular classroom teacher	
		Teacher of gifted children	
	Collection of additional information (work samples, anecdotal reports, interest inventories)	Teacher of handicapped children	
		Parents	
	Interpretation of results	Child	

Educational Assessment for IEP Development			
Review of identification information	Administrator		Determination of educational goals, objectives, and means by which they are to be accomplished
Administration of educational mastery tests	Regular classroom teacher		
Administration of interest inventories	Teacher of gifted children		
Determination of preferred sensory modality	Teacher of handicapped children		
Determination of learning mode preferences (e.g., programed instruction, small group activities)	Parents		
	Child		
Summary of results			

1978; Maker, 1977), since affective problems constitute an obstacle to academic and personal development.

The superior power of observation which is characteristic of gifted children may bring an early and deeply felt awareness of the stigma associated with many handicapping conditions. These children are quicker than other handicapped children to notice the discomfort and lowered expectations that many people experience with the handicapped. Consequently, it is not surprising that many gifted handicapped adults report low self concept as a major problem in their educational and social development (Maker, 1977). These adults offered the following suggestions which teachers can use to promote emotional adjustment.

1. Encourage artistic pursuits which can provide emotional release.
2. Provide opportunities to deal with feelings about being handicapped.
3. Provide opportunities to interact with nonhandicapped people.
4. Offer counseling services.

Parental involvement is vital to the emotional and intellectual development of gifted handicapped students. Early identification and training for parents may forestall overprotective attitudes which discourage the risk taking behaviors needed for growth. Parents and teachers of the gifted handicapped should encourage them to test their intellectual, physical, and social limits. An atmosphere of support and encouragement can free them to make mistakes and learn from them.

Teacher Inservice

All teachers involved in the instruction of gifted handicapped children will need inservice training. However, all of them will also *be* inservice trainers. The gifted education teacher has knowledge and skills which can be taught to the teacher of handicapped children, and vice versa. For example, the gifted education teacher can help the regular classroom teacher and the teacher of handicapped children learn and use educational models which can be used to teach productive thinking skills. Guilford's Structure of Intellect Model (Guilford, 1967) may be especially useful for teaching and testing gifted handicapped children because it encourages consideration of many specific abilities. The uneven ability profile characteristic of many gifted handicapped children suggests the usefulness of this model.

The teacher of handicapped children can offer instruction on developmental and ability patterns characteristic of the various categories of handicapping conditions. The regular classroom teacher and teacher of the gifted program will also need information on alternative modes of instruction for handicapped children and learning aids which facilitate mastery of advanced content despite physical, sensory, or learning disabilities. For example, the teacher of handicapped children can provide information on materials such as audiotapes or large print versions of advanced textbooks which may be used with visually impaired children or with learning disabled children who have visual perception problems.

SUMMARY OF ISSUES IN PROGRAM DEVELOPMENT AND IMPLEMENTATION

Although there is still much to be learned about how to educate children who have exceptional ability in some areas and exceptional deficits in others, there is a sufficient knowledge base to support development and implementation of programs for gifted handicapped children. As in any effort to bring about institutional change, input from people who will be affected by the change should be obtained at every level of planning. The preceding sections have pointed out the involvement of professional personnel and parents in screening, identification, and educational planning and instruction. The following administrative issues and questions are designed to highlight the need for early and continued broad-based involvement in efforts to meet the needs of children who challenge our ability to combine expertise and resources.

1. Policy and procedures
   a. Have I formed a committee representing administrative, instructional and support personnel and parents of the gifted handicapped to review the literature as well as local policy and procedures for the gifted and for the handicapped?
   b. Has my district or state adopted policy and procedures regarding the education of the gifted handicapped?
   c. Does my state or district have a process by which suggested policy and procedures can be reviewed by appropriate personnel?

2. Programing
   a. Has my district formed a task force of instructional personnel to review the literature, consult with experts to identify model instructional programs, methods, and materials suitable for use with gifted handicapped children?
   b. Does my state or district have procedures for making recommendations to administrative personnel regarding programing for gifted handicapped students?

3. Personnel development
   a. Does my State Department of Education provide training for administrators, teachers, and other personnel on the gifted handicapped?
   b. Does my state or district provide awareness, training, and counseling services to parents of gifted handicapped children?

SAMPLE IEP

Child's Name: *David Martin*
School: *Lake Elementary*
Grade: *Fourth*
Date of Program Entry: *October 1, 1980*
Prioritized Annual Goals:
1. To complete assigned classwork.
2. To improve reading comprehension and word attack skills.
3. To improve verbal creativity, especially fluency and elaboration.
4. To develop mechanical ability.
5. To develop understanding of basic elements of electronics.

Short Term Instructional Objectives	Specific Educational and/or Support Services
1a. David will complete 5 of 10 class assignments.	Behavior modification program, where David will explore different methods of completing assignments (oral, written, taped, etc.) and gradually increase the length of assignment.
b. David will complete 8 of 10 class assignments.	
c. David will complete all class assignments.	
2a. David will be able to identify the main idea and major concepts in reading passages at the third grade level with 90% accuracy.	Individualized program in word attack skills.
b. David will learn word attack skills needed to read fluently at the third grade level.	Individualized program in word attack skills.
c. David will master words on the Dolch basic reading vocabulary list.	Individualized reading vocabulary program.
3a. Given a divergent thinking task, David will add at least five elaborative details.	Participation in divergent thinking activities in the gifted resource room.

**Summary of Present Levels of
Performance:**

Strengths:
    Spatial reasoning and memory
    Verbal reasoning
    Mechanical ability
    Interest in electronics
Weaknesses:
    Failure to complete assignments
    Reading comprehension and word attack skills
    Creative thinking skills, especially fluency and elaboration

Person(s) Responsible	Review Date	Mastery	Non-mastery
Classroom teacher and learning disabilities teacher	Quarterly	_____	_____
	Quarterly	_____	_____
	Quarterly	_____	_____
Learning disabilities teacher	Quarterly	_____	_____
Learning disabilities teacher	Quarterly	_____	_____
Learning disabilities teacher	Quarterly	_____	_____
Gifted resource teacher	Quarterly	_____	_____

SAMPLE IEP (continued)

Short Term Instructional Objectives	Specific Educational and/or Support Services
b. Given a verbal divergent thinking task, David will add at least 10 elaborative details and increase the number of ideas by 10%.	Participation in divergent thinking activities in the gifted resource room.
c. Given a verbal divergent thinking task, David will add at least 15 elaborative details and increase the number of ideas by 10%.	Participation in divergent thinking activities in the gifted resource room.
4a. David will be able to complete a teacher-made test of basic addition and subtraction skills with 100% accuracy.	Individualized math program in the regular classroom.
b. David will be able to complete a teacher-made test of multiplication skills with 95% accuracy.	Individualized math program in the regular classroom.
c. David will be able to complete a teacher-made test of division skills with 95% accuracy.	Individualized math program in the regular classroom.
5a. David will be able to assemble a code practice oscillator, a crystal diode radio, and a three transistor radio.	Instruction in the gifted resource room.
b. David will be able to assemble a wireless AM transmitter, a tone modulated transmitter, and a radio operated switch.	Instruction in the gifted resource room.
c. David will be able to assemble a code checker, an audio signal tester, and a DC bridge rectifier.	Instruction in the gifted resource room.

SAMPLE IEP (continued)

Person(s) Responsible	Review Date	Mastery	Non-mastery
Gifted resource teacher	Quarterly	_____	_____
Gifted resource teacher	Quarterly	_____	_____
Classroom teacher	Quarterly	_____	_____
Classroom teacher	Quarterly	_____	_____
Classroom teacher	Quarterly	_____	_____
Gifted resource teacher	Quarterly	_____	_____
Gifted resource teacher	Quarterly	_____	_____
Gifted resource teacher	Quarterly	_____	_____

SAMPLE IEP (continued)

Short Term Instructional Objectives	Specific Educational and/or Support Services
6a. David will be able to complete a test of radio theory terminology with at least 90% accuracy.	Instruction in basic radio theory terminology.
b. David will be able to send and receive Morse code at a speed of at least 5 words per minute.	Practice in Morse code.
c. David will pass the FCC test for a novice radio license. (Test will be given orally.)	Instruction in principles of basic radio theory.
d. David will demonstrate increased positive feelings about his own self worth as measured by his responses on the Tennessee Self Concept Inventory.	Counseling and activities designed to promote a positive self concept.

Special Education and Related Services to be Delivered:

Resource room for gifted children for 2 hours a day, 5 days per week.

Resource room for learning disabled children for 1 hour a day, 3 days per week.

Counseling: 1 day per week.

Committee Members Present:

David Martin *(student)*
M/M Edward Martin *(parents)*
Rosemary Liddell *(principal)*
Maria Viaforte *(classroom teacher)*
Larry Bronson *(gifted resource teacher)*

Dates of Meeting: *9/2/80; 9/15/80*

SAMPLE IEP (continued)

Person(s) Responsible	Review Date	Mastery	Non-mastery
Gifted resource teacher	Quarterly	————	————
Gifted resource teacher	Quarterly	————	————
Volunteer from local amateur radio club	Quarterly	————	————
Parents, classroom teacher, and counselor	Quarterly	————	————

Committee Recommendations for Specific Procedures/Techniques, Materials (Include information about learning style.)

David's expressed interests which might be helpful in developing a reinforcement "menu" are building model cars and airplanes, reading mechanics and electronics magazines, using a microscope, and browsing in the library.

He prefers working alone, working on a one to one basis with an adult, or working in small groups. Oral instruction, individualized learning packages, and independent or small group investigation should accommodate David's preferred learning styles.

David's long history of failure to complete assignments suggests that this will be a difficult habit for him to overcome. He should be rewarded for small increments in improvement in this area in at least the initial stages of his program. Emphasis on fluency and elaboration of ideas is important

SAMPLE IEP (continued)

because part of David's problem in completing assignments seems to be lack of ability or lack of willingness to generate ideas and elaborate on them. Individualized commercial or teacher-made arithmetic materials concentrating on computational skills are available in the materials center. The local amateur radio club has materials on basic radio theory. The president of the club has offered his services as a mentor for students who are interested in amateur radio.

Objective Evaluation Criteria for Each Annual Goal Statement:

The criteria for mastery of the last objective in the sequence of objectives related to each annual goal statement constitutes criteria for mastery of the goal. The person responsible for the implementation of objectives related to each goal will be responsible for evaluation and for reporting progress to the committee on each of the review dates.

REFERENCES

Grossi, J. A. *Model state policy, legislation and state plan toward the education of gifted and talented students.* Reston VA: The Council for Exceptional Children, 1980.

Guilford, J. P. *The nature of human intelligence.* New York: McGraw-Hill, 1967.

Leonard, J. *Chapel Hill services to the gifted-handicapped: A project summary.* Chapel Hill NC: Chapel Hill Training-Outreach Project, 1978.

Maker, C. J. *Providing programs for the gifted-handicapped.* Reston VA: The Council for Exceptional Children, 1977.

Mercer, J. R., & Lewis, J. F. Using the system of multicultural pluralistic assessment (SOMPA) to identify the gifted minority child. In Baldwin, A. Y., Gear, G. H., & Lucito, L. J. (Eds.), *Educational planning for the gifted: Overcoming cultural, geographic, and socioeconomic barriers.* Reston VA: The Council for Exceptional Children, 1978.

Renzulli, J. S. *The enrichment triad model: A guide for developing defensible programs for the gifted and talented.* Wethersfield CT: Creative Learning Press, 1977.

Renzulli, J. S., & Smith, L. H. *A guidebook for developing individualized educational programs (IEP) for gifted and talented students.* Wethersfield CT: Creative Learning Press, 1979.

Terman, L. M., & Oden, M. The gifted child grows up. In *Genetic studies of genius* (Vol. IV). Stanford CA: Stanford University Press, 1947.

White, A. *Project SEARCH: Phase II evaluation.* New Haven CT: Project SEARCH, 1976.

- Parents who are involved in the gifted or talented child's educational program are its best advocates.
- Parents involved in the educational program of their child are in the best position to form a local parent group.
- The school can put the parent in touch with resources in the community, county, or state that will meet the special needs of the gifted child or the child's family.

As a prerequisite to any collaborative effort, the administrator makes a firm commitment to working with parents of the gifted and talented, and assumes the role of catalyst in promoting this commitment within the school district. A self examination of philosophy and approach to working with parents may lead the administrator to pose the following questions:

- Do I acknowledge the parent's right to be involved?
- Do I see the family as a focus of my school or district's service?
- Do I believe that parents have a right to share in the establishment of goals and objectives for their child's education?
- Can I be flexible in providing multiple options for family participation, realizing that no one strategy is appropriate for all?
- Can I be open to whatever level of involvement a family chooses, and yet remain supportive?
- Do I see the positives in parents and practice positive reinforcement?
- Do I help families use and develop community resources as needed?
- Do I help provide opportunities for parents and other family members to learn about child development and acquire specific skills to work with their children at home?

Depending upon the administrator's answers to these questions, the information presented in this chapter may serve to reinforce existing practices or provide assistance in making the parent/administrator relationship more rewarding. This chapter explores the concerns of parents of gifted and talented children, and outlines techniques and strategies designed to build stronger parent/administrator partnerships. Suggestions and activities presented have already been successfully implemented or are based on sound educational theory and practice.

THE CASE FOR COLLABORATION

Administrators are in a unique position to nurture positive and helpful parent/teacher relationships. They recognize that both parent and teacher are in teaching/learning situations. Each observes and interacts with the child, but in different environments. Observations made and information collected by each are valuable in forming a comprehensive profile of the

CHAPTER 9

Parents and Administrators:
Working Together

JOHN A. GROSSI

Fostering positive working relationships requires a substantial expenditure of time and effort by both parents and administrators. An effective program of parent involvement is one initiated by school personnel who regard parents as an essential element of the educational service delivery system. They concur that the development of a program to involve parents must be stated as an accepted goal of the school district, with progress toward achievement viewed as a continuing process (Coletta, 1977).

COMMITMENT TO PARTNERSHIP

The foundation of a parent/administrator partnership is based on certain assumptions which underscore the need for schools and parents to work together. As suggested by Karnes (in press), these assumptions include the following:

- The home is the institution that has major influence on the child's values, attitudes, and behavior and should help to determine what the child's educational program should be.
- The family usually knows more about the interests and needs of the gifted child than anyone else and should share this information with teachers so that it can be utilized in educational programing.
- Family members can learn a great deal from teachers or caretakers of the gifted or talented child and can reinforce what the school is fostering at home.

child that includes a full range of interests and abilities. This profile, in turn, will facilitate the development and implementation of an appropriate educational plan.

Traditionally the relationship between parents and school administrators has been characterized as one of protagonism/antagonism. Although both are dedicated to improving educational services, their differing perspectives often serve to block the realization of their common goals. Employment of dissimilar strategies has often caused tension, annoyance, and distrust between the two groups, resulting in disjointed and sometimes unsuccessful efforts to facilitate the establishment of sound educational programs and services.

In the area of gifted and talented education, this adversary relationship has been particularly intense. Many parents, realizing that their children have unique learning abilities, are frustrated to find no avenue of expression or challenge within their local public school system. Many, however, are no longer willing to accept a *laissez-faire* attitude on the part of the schools, and are demanding increased attention to the educational requirements of the gifted and talented. Intensified advocacy has, in some instances, created an atmosphere of conflict and confrontation between parents and school personnel, making existing schisms and differences even more pronounced.

Administrators, too, face their own unique frustrations. Overwhelmed in recent years by state and federal mandates to develop policies and establish programs for the education of other populations of special needs students, many are reluctant to commit limited energy and resources to the gifted and talented. Others are unfamiliar with the special educational needs of these children and are hesitant to explore the administrative and educational procedures appropriate for this student population.

Parents have been popularly perceived by many educators as relatively disinterested in their children's education, as well as unequipped with the skills needed to assist in teaching. Parents of the gifted and talented, on the other hand, have traditionally been their children's strongest and most vocal advocates (Karnes, in press). They often formulate educational goals and objectives for their children independent of school input. Through communication and collaboration, school administrators as major providers of educational services should participate actively rather than be excluded from this process.

Because public education for the gifted and talented has been underdeveloped, parents have often taken the initiative to provide educational supplementation, ranging from identification to actual service delivery. In such instances, the school is placed in a secondary rather than primary position of service provider. Direct involvement has given parents an acute sensitivity to the educational, social, and emotional needs of their children, making them more aware of their rights and responsibilities as parents, as well as more assertive in exercising those rights.

Parents of the gifted and talented have now and will continue to have in the future a vested interest in and a definite impact on the education of their children. Their involvement in the development and implementation of school programs for the gifted and talented is a natural outgrowth of this reality. School administrators determined to establish and maintain effective programs will seek to sensitize themselves to the concerns of parents and establish a positive working relationship with this constituency.

Parental involvement is a natural resource available to the schools. In the past, the degree of parental involvement in ongoing school programs has often been determined by the amount of money available for its support. Yet it is precisely the present constraints of energy and resources at both federal and state levels which point to the benefits inherent in viewing parents in more of a resource capacity. Administrators will need to solicit their active support in the implementation of successful programs for the gifted and talented.

In situations where parents and the schools have worked together to pool their collective talents, all parties have reaped substantial benefits. To achieve the harmonious and collaborative atmosphere necessary to provide quality education, administrators will take steps to involve parents of the gifted and talented in those decisions and operations affecting their children's education. Both parents and administrators must redirect their energies toward positive collaboration.

Coordinating activities to accomplish these goals, however, is only one facet of the responsibility assumed by administrators. Parents are entitled to services and support whether or not the desired collaboration has been established. Offering such support will contribute to the establishment of a positive working relationship for the future.

INVOLVING PARENTS IN THE SCHOOL PROGRAM

In order to facilitate the creative and active involvement of parents in all aspects of the gifted and talented program, the administrator will seek not only to include parents in specific activities but also pave the way within the school system for the establishment of procedures and policies governing this aspect of school programing. The administrator will want to promote policies that are flexible enough to govern multiple programmatic options and encourage total family participation.

Traditionally, the schools have welcomed parent participation on largely a passive level. Parents are invited to visit the school at a designated time to observe and react to end products of completed school or classroom activities. Certainly this approach is an appropriate means of involving parents. However, it is only one of a variety of more creative alternatives.

Passive involvement deprives the school of needed assistance and denies the children a comprehensive education (Pennsylvania Department of Education, 1973).

In a school system that has an ongoing program for the gifted and talented, administrators will focus on at least two major areas: meeting the educational needs of the children, and meeting the information and awareness needs of parents. Kaufman (1976) has suggested some activities administrators may employ to meet those objectives.

- *Newsletters.* A newsletter sent from the school to the parents may contain a potpourri of information concerning the education of the gifted and talented and related issues that have an impact on that student population.

- *Parent Handbook.* The school or district may wish to compile a handbook explaining the purpose of the gifted and talented program, procedures employed by the schools in identifying children who are gifted and talented, differential approaches to curricula, and program evaluation strategies. The handbook may also include information on programs that encourage parent involvement, as well as other ways a parent may volunteer time to assist the school in achieving program goals and objectives.

- *Classroom Observation.* Encouraging parents to make classroom observations will provide parents with a firsthand view of classroom and school operations, teaching strategies, student behavior, and level of discipline difficulty. Multiple rather than single observations will help the parent obtain a more comprehensive view of the student, the teacher, and the school.

- *Small and Large Group Meetings.* Administrators who make themselves available to parents as often as possible will alleviate potential problems while at the same time demonstrating empathy and a genuine show of support. Small meetings conducted for one or a very few parents to discuss and work through problems and concerns of a highly specific nature are beneficial. However, large group meetings are also helpful if the issues at hand are of concern to many parents.

- *Field Trips.* Field trips can be one of the most exciting, creative, and worthwhile learning experiences available to children. Parental involvement can ease some of the planning and supervision difficulties that often make school personnel reluctant to undertake field trips. Inviting parents to assist in the planning and organization of the outing will help solidify parent/school relationships and further reinforce the total educational program for the gifted and talented. Parents who accompany students in a supervisory capacity free the teacher to concentrate on the learning aspects of the field trip.

- *Theory and/or Strategy Courses for Parents.* Courses that explore the global characteristics of gifted and talented children, their educational needs, educational theories for meeting those needs, and strategies for implementation may be sponsored by either the schools, state education agencies, or state or local institutions of higher education. Such courses are an invaluable resource for parents, and in addition to easing the fears or uncertainties many parents have concerning their children, will also nurture good relationships between parents and the schools.

- *Home Activity Sheets.* The preparation and distribution of home activity sheets for parents to use with their gifted child will maintain and supplement the continuity of the school program. These activities will continue the teaching efforts made during the school day. For parents who experience some anxiety about their ability to carry out supplementary activities, the schools may offer informal training and technical assistance.

In order to sensitize and inform parents in a firsthand manner of the operation and coordination necessary to run a school, school site visits can also be a valuable experience. Parents will develop a better understanding of the diverse educational approaches and responsibilities of school personnel. An orientation session will help parents make more acute observations of ongoing school functions necessary to the understanding of the total plant operation. The superintendent of schools or other official may be available prior to the actual visit to discuss programs and plans for the gifted and talented and their relative priority within the school district. If programs for the gifted and talented exist within the school system, parents may visit them and talk to building principals and teachers. If a system has no such programs, visits to neighboring systems may be arranged as an alternative activity.

STRATEGIES FOR WORKING WITH PARENT GROUPS

The involvement of administrators and other school and district personnel in the formation of a parent advocate association for the gifted and talented offers a variety of benefits that address several areas of potential difficulty. Such an association gives the administrator a way of offering the attention and consideration expected and deserved by parents, which is difficult to provide individually because of time and schedule constraints. Parent associations also provide a forum for the administrator to communicate accurate information concerning the school or district situation, thus facilitating understanding and helping parents put their demands in perspective. School involvement in a parent association may help to eliminate many preestablished mindsets, thus removing barriers to successful parent/administrator collaboration.

Most importantly, such participation demonstrates support for parents and offers a means of expanding the school's resources through the use of an often untapped pool of talent. Rather than viewing the parent association as a monitoring group dictating the types and extent of services that the schools should provide to gifted children, collaborative involvement in its formation will establish the framework for a mutually supportive relationship.

Administrators may assist parents at every phase of the development of an effective parent organization. Niro (1976) has identified steps for parents to follow in the development of an association. Suggestions for collaborative administrator input are presented to parallel each phase of this development.

- *Parents*: Publicize
- *Administrators*:

  Inschool Dissemination. A simple information handout sent home with each child will inform a large number of parents of the interest in beginning a parent organization. Those parents who feel the need to improve the educational offerings available to gifted and talented children will not overlook this invitation.

  Local News Media. Community newspapers are always anxious to cover local schools for potential articles. As such, school administrators are often in a better position than parents to attract the local media. A press release briefly explaining the intent to establish a local parent group for the gifted and talented can be disseminated to newspapers throughout the community for placement in the "community news section." This announcement will help to reach parents who do not have children in school, or those who did not receive the announcement sent from the school. Following is an example of a simple and succinct press release that conveys the intended message clearly.

Dr. John Smith, principal of Edgeview Elementary School, is interested in helping to establish a parent association for gifted and talented children. Dr. Smith would like to meet with parents and others interested in forming such a group at the Newton Community Center on Wednesday, January 13, 1981 at 8:00 p.m. Persons interested in pursuing this matter but who cannot meet on January 13, are asked to call Dr. Smith at 703-860-1543.

PTA. An announcement to the PTA of the intent to form a parent association for the gifted and talented will reach an even broader audience. The presence of a school administrator at a PTA meeting for this purpose is particularly effective.

- *Parents:* Identify membership
- *Administrators:* By keeping school staff informed and encouraging them to become members, the schools will not only assist in the identification of new members, but also provide balance to the membership and promote a more comprehensive approach to the education of gifted and talented students. Invitations to membership may also be placed in established school and district newsletters and other written communications.

- *Parents:* Affiliation
- *Administrators*: Because of the nature of their positions and the opportunity for travel throughout the district and state, school administrators are often aware of other organizations with the same or similar objectives as the parent association. Sharing that information with parents is one way of facilitating affiliation with related organizations.

- *Parents*: Choosing a name
- *Administrators*: The name selected for the parent organization is of critical importance. Individual members shift and change, but the name remains as an important statement of identity and philosophy. The name selected should reflect the interests of the group and the types of persons who comprise its membership. The school administrator who wants the organization to embrace the joint concerns of both parents and schools should have input in selecting an organizational name that reflects this intent.

- *Parents:* Meetings
- *Administrators*: In the course of business travel throughout the state, the administrator may serve as the organization representative at meetings or seminars sponsored by organizations of related purpose or interest. Such contacts may further provide a source of speakers for association meetings. The school administrator may also make a school building available for the parent association to conduct its meetings.

A parent group may initiate surveys to determine the number and needs of gifted and talented students in the community. Such a mutual undertaking can serve as a worthwhile organizational activity (Delp & Martinson, 1975), and can benefit both administrators and parents. Surveys conducted jointly by parents and the schools will have a much greater impact than those conducted by either group separately. Data collected can yield information about community resources, determine what services already exist, and identify persons who can help with unmet needs. A survey may also explore the possibility of developing private sector resources to start or expand programs. Cooperative ventures can also be undertaken, resulting in the establishment of linkages with parent groups in neighboring communities to receive program suggestions and general moral support.

Communication with the state education agency, while often overlooked, is a particularly effective method of furthering the scope of a parent organization. Joint communication will keep parents and administrators apprised of state efforts and activities in the area of gifted education, and provide the state with information necessary for important decision making. The state education agency can provide the parent association with information concerning legislation, funding, programs, other parent groups and their activities, agencies which provide services for the gifted and talented, and sources for materials to be disseminated to members.

EXEMPLARY PARENT INITIATED PROGRAMS

Parent initiated activities often result in significant benefit to the school, the parents, and most importantly, the children. The following programs are illustrative of successful parent/school collaboration originated by parents. (See Chapter 14 for a partial listing of names and addresses of parent/ advocate groups, arranged by state.)

Adults for Gifted and Talented Education (AGATE): Loudoun County, Virginia

1. *Enrichment Program, Grades 1–3:* AGATE proposed this program to fill the void of a lack of services for the gifted and talented in the primary grades. AGATE parents have been given total responsibility for the design and operation of an enrichment program in several county schools.

2. *Mentors in the Schools:* Perceiving a need for a mentorship program in the local high schools, AGATE representatives identify students and mentors, establish required matches, and coordinate transportation. The schools support this program through the allocation of funds for expenses.

3. *Visibility in the Schools:* AGATE parents make a concerted effort to be present in the schools on a regular basis through volunteer efforts. In addition to providing needed assistance, their presence within eye and ear shot of school personnel increases the effectiveness of their input in school programs.

Program for the Enrichment of the Gifted (PEG): Prince William County, Virginia

1. *Student Visitations:* Gifted students from surrounding counties and districts who have been involved in creative projects are invited to share their experiences with other students, parents, teachers, and administrators. PEG finances and coordinates all arrangements, and provides lodging in members' homes for those students who travel long distances. The schools provide facilities and transportation.
2. *Stipends*: PEG awards stipends to teachers and administrators to attend local conferences for the gifted and talented.
3. *Field Trips:* Field trips that are judged to be worthwhile are given financial support by PEG.

Michigan Association for the Academically Talented, Inc. (MAAT)

1. *Community Advisory Committees*: MAAT members sit on community advisory committees that provide input and direction to school personnel in the education of gifted and talented children. They react to established educational plans and work to assure the inclusion of gifted and talented students in all aspects of school programing.
2. *Newsletters:* MAAT disseminates a newsletter to all public schools within the state to inform school personnel of the organization's activities and encourage participation.

Gifted Child Society: Oakland, New Jersey

1. *Saturday Enrichment Programs:* The Gifted Child Society supports extensive course offerings in many diverse areas for gifted and talented students. Local school personnel often teach these courses.
2. *Training:* Training sessions for parents and school administrators on issues related to the gifted and talented are offered in addition to inservice training provided by the schools.
3. *Publications:* The Gifted Child Society is responsible for a number of publications on the gifted and talented as well as the establishment and maintenance of a parent association.

TRAINING PARENTS IN THE LEGISLATIVE PROCESS

Legislation which determines the direction of local, state, and federal activities in the area of gifted and talented education is fundamental. Periodically, this legislation is reauthorized. At such times, a state or the federal government may strengthen or weaken its legislative policy base and its appropriations to implement legislation.

Parents can and should play a major role in policy development. In those instances where the gifted and talented have made legislative advances, parents have been a major force. School administrators can assist and strengthen parent advocacy by providing opportunities for parents to acquire political skills and undertake activities that will effect legislation for the gifted and talented. Grossi (1980) has outlined a number of strategies for training parents to become active participants in the legislative process.

Information Sharing

Initiating and maintaining open and constant communication with their elected representatives is the most effective way for parents to influence legislation. Because elected officials represent all constituents, not just special interest groups, communication to a representative should deal with pressing legislative issues and should include information that serves to clarify and nurture a given position. Effective parent groups are those that are well informed about the issues surrounding the education of gifted and talented children, and can furnish specific content information to elected representatives at all levels of government.

Drafting a Bill

A parent group can draft a bill sensitive to the needs of the gifted and talented children throughout a given state, and then seek a sponsor from among their elected representatives.

Technical Assistance

Parents can contact a professional advocate organization for technical assistance in determining a direction and selecting a set of strategies to influence legislation.

Letter Writing

Whether undertaken by individuals or groups, letters help officials identify voter sentiment on major issues. Legislators appreciate letters that are well thought out and clearly represent a particular point of view. The content should be explanatory without being wordy. Form letters carry little weight compared to individually worded communications.

Telephone Calls

This strategy is useful for short range activities and immediate input. When telephoning a representative's office, callers should identify themselves and their affiliation, such as parent of a gifted and talented child, or member of a specific parent organization. If the legislator is out of the office, a staff member will forward all information to the legislator.

Sending Wires

On the day a bill is due to be acted upon, sending a wire encouraging representative support is most effective. Wires should be short and to the point, generally no more than three typewritten lines.

Visitations

A personal visit to a representative's office requires a greater commitment of time and energy, but is particularly effective because it allows the representative to identify an issue more personally with a specific group or individual.

Testifying

Parents may offer testimony at scheduled legislative hearings to present a case for gifted and talented children.

School administrators may assist parents in their advocacy efforts by sensitizing legislators and other policy makers to the educational needs of the gifted and talented. Effective strategies include the following:

- Inviting legislators to visit classrooms or programs for the gifted and talented.
- Inviting legislators as speakers or guests at organization banquets, meetings, or other functions.
- Recognizing legislators who have publicly advocated for the gifted and talented through awards or letters of thanks.
- Publicizing relevant activities involving legislators in local newspapers and on radio and television.

SUMMARY

Administrators intent on designing and implementing programs for the gifted and talented will give serious consideration to expanding their traditional roles and exploring new and innovative approaches. There is no substitute for creativity and originality. Administrators should not hesitate to try new things. Whatever the degree of success, their efforts will demonstrate a commitment to provide and strengthen educational programs and services for gifted and talented children and their parents.

REFERENCES

Coletta, A. J. *Working together: A guide to parent involvement.* Atlanta: Humanities Limited, 1977.

Delp, J., & Martinson, R. *The gifted and talented: A handbook for parents.* Reston VA: The Council for Exceptional Children, 1975.

Ginsberg, G., & Harrison, C. H. *How to help your gifted child, a handbook for parents and teachers.* New York: Monarch Press, 1977.

Grossi, J. A. *How a parent group can effect legislation for the gifted and talented.* Reston VA: The Council for Exceptional Children, 1980.

Karnes, M. B. Involving the family in the development of the young gifted and talented. In M. B. Karnes (Ed.), *Identifying and programing for the young gifted/talented.* Reston VA: The Council for Exceptional Children, in press.

Kaufman, F. *Your gifted child and you.* Reston VA: The Council for Exceptional Children, 1976.

Niro, L. D. *Forming a local parent association for gifted and talented education.* Reston VA: The Council for Exceptional Children, 1976.

Pennsylvania Department of Education. *A guide for parents: Mentally gifted children and youth.* Harrisburg PA: Bureau of Special and Compensatory Education, 1973.

CHAPTER 10

Criteria for the Selection of Materials

JOYCE VAN TASSEL

Selection of materials appropriate to the needs of gifted students and to the specific gifted program plan is a critical component in good program management. While materials are not the basis of the program, they can provide a helpful framework for both students and teachers.

Curriculum planning and development involve careful decision making on the part of gifted program coordinators over a period of time. Selecting materials is only one part of that process, and should be considered in the context of the following content approaches.

CONTENT APPROACHES

A universe of possibilities is reflected in the content approaches currently adopted in gifted programs. These programs can be categorized according to five types.

Traditional Content Acceleration Programs

These programs are typically in core academic areas such as math, science, and reading/language arts. They incorporate a faster pace and greater depth for gifted students within that area. Examples are science courses at The Bronx High School of Science, advanced placement courses at many high schools in a variety of academic areas, and the Junior Great Books program organized in many elementary districts.

Process Programs

These programs are built on the rationale that gifted students should develop important skills that can be applied to all content areas. Many districts have adopted programs in critical thinking, creative thinking, research and independent study skills, and rational decision making. Few packaged programs exist in this area other than the fine Purdue Creative Thinking Program, although many workbooks in these skill areas are available.

Independent Mode Programs

These programs adopt the premise that gifted students should be encouraged to be independent learners at an early age and to a greater extent than other students. Examples of such programs are internships (e.g., the Executive Internship Program), mentorships, and two important program models: Feldhusen's Purdue Three-Stage Enrichment Model (Feldhusen & Kolloff, 1978) and Renzulli's Enrichment Triad (Renzulli, 1977). A popular and sometimes mandatory organizational approach to this kind of program is the use of an individualized education program (IEP) which provides documentation of student assessment data and educational recommendations for growth in any number of areas.

Multidisciplinary Programs

These programs build on the ability of gifted children to understand interrelationships and grasp meanings more readily than the average child. Examples include humanities programs and technology programs which incorporate computer science with other fields. The Astor Program in New York City is a good example of a multidisciplinary program at the preschool level.

Enrichment Programs

Although the term *enrichment* is troublesome to define, its use in this context refers to "new" content areas to which the gifted have not previously been exposed in the regular school curriculum, but which represent, by their very nature, challenging content. Examples include courses in law, such as the program developed at Chelmsford, Massachusetts; courses in logic such as the one in Plainsfield, New Jersey; and philosophy courses such as the program developed at Montclair State College in New Jersey. The upsurge of interest in the teaching of foreign languages to the gifted is another example of this kind of enrichment. Long running gifted programs such as those in Cleveland and Indianapolis have never abandoned it, however.

ORGANIZING PRINCIPLES

Once a content approach has been selected, it must be organized in such a way as to maximize the abilities and potential of gifted students. Numerous gifted programs employ organizing principles such as the following:

1. Bloom's taxonomy, at the levels of analysis, synthesis, and evaluation (Bloom, 1969)
2. Guilford's Structure of the Intellect (Meeker, 1969)
3. Model for Implementing Cognitive and Affective Behavior (Williams, 1970)
4. The Purdue Three-Stage Enrichment Model (Feldhusen & Kolloff, 1978)
5. Renzulli's Enrichment Triad (Renzulli, 1977)

TEACHING STRATEGIES

All gifted programs need to employ good teaching strategies, some of which are more conducive to certain kinds of programs than to others. For example, inquiry teaching is an effective technique in social studies and English (courses in which discussion is a key component), while it may not be as helpful in foreign languages or mathematics where application of skills is stressed.

In the final analysis, strategies for working with the gifted are more heavily predicated on understanding their needs than on demonstrating special techniques. At a minimum, however, teachers of the gifted should have in their arsenal the ability to do inquiry teaching, ask good discussion questions, organize small groups and independent work, and lecture effectively and efficiently.

Other teaching strategies for use with gifted students include lecture, group discussion, independent study, modeling/demonstration, simulations/games, programed instruction, inquiry, experiential (classroom/lab based), materials utilization, community based practicum, drill and recitation, peer projects, and problem solving (creative/critical). A curriculum development model such as the one presented in Figure 1 can best reflect the relationship of materials to the overall curriculum planning process as it might be carried out in a school setting.

MATERIALS FOR GIFTED STUDENTS

Most materials for gifted students can be categorized into five types: mastery level and/or proficiency materials in traditional content areas; critical and creative thinking skill materials; materials constructed around a theoretical model; interdisciplinary materials; and potpourri, materials that constitute random and unrelated activities loosely termed *gifted*.

FIGURE 1
Curriculum Development for
Gifted/Talented

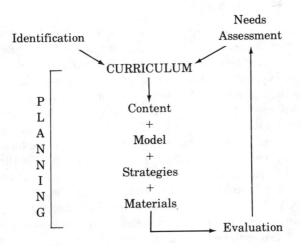

Mastery Level Materials

Since most gifted programs tend to focus on traditional content areas, it is essential to place special emphasis on collecting mastery level materials within those content areas. Textbook purchases have been geared to reading levels slightly below age norms, and the discrepancy in grade level material is even greater than thought at first blush for these students.

When the term *mastery level material* is used in relation to the gifted, it implies that the reading level is slightly above their actual proficiency in order to ensure room for challenge and growth. In addition, mastery level materials encourage a student to go beyond the minimum through examining topics in greater depth and broader scope.

Thinking Skill Materials

In the last five years, many materials have been published which address "thinking" as a separate content area to be taught. Activities structured around deductive thinking skills, analogies, and aspects of language such as synonyms, antonyms, and patterns are examples. Much of this type of material is in workbook form and can be used by individual students or small groups. Both verbal and figural exercises are available, as are creative thinking workbooks.

The use of critical and creative thinking materials is an important part of any good gifted program, and should be included within the selected content focus. It is rather difficult, however, to plan an entire gifted program around thinking skills without application to content beyond what the available materials provide.

Theoretical Model Materials

Many teacher made and commercial materials are based on two popular theoretical models that have been adapted for use with the gifted. One of these is J. P. Guilford's Structure of the Intellect (Guilford, 1967); the other, Bloom's taxonomy (Bloom, 1969). In each case, abstract mental manipulations that are arbitrarily labeled serve as the basis for constructing activities. For example, the manipulation of drawing implications is addressed through structuring a series of scenarios in which students make hypotheses regarding situations and relate them to real life constructs.

The organization of such activities is usually determined by the levels of the model. Activities constructed around Bloom's taxonomy, for example, are structured from descending to ascending order in knowledge, comprehension, application, analysis, synthesis, and evaluation.

In both cases, process rather than content is the focus for materials development. The usefulness of such materials depends to a great extent on the focus of the program. Teacher constructed materials within specific content areas using these models may be very good, depending on the level of understanding of the teachers involved. Certainly a strong grounding in at least one content area is necessary in order to manipulate the models appropriately.

Materials currently available using these models are appropriate for supplementary use in a gifted program. Unless carefully selected, these materials become random in their application and sporadic in their benefit.

Interdisciplinary Materials

Selection of interdisciplinary materials that offer scope and depth is essential if the field of gifted education expects to advance in its approach to appropriate curriculum. Such materials attempt to provide thematic, historical, or underlying logical systems as a framework in which to fit all bodies of knowledge, thus providing students with an understanding of how incidental pieces of knowledge fit together across content areas. The level of such materials often implies limiting their use to teacher reference, although portions can be adapted for direct student use. All gifted programs could profit from the increased use of such material.

Potpourri Materials

Spurred on by increased interest in the field of gifted education, commercial publishers and others have glutted the market with a potpourri of activities for gifted students. The main problem with many of these materials is that they are not structured in such a way that a gifted program could be built around them, nor are they effective in ongoing programs since they lack the basic criteria for gifted materials discussed in the following section. Perhaps their best use is for the regular classroom teacher who wants an isolated creative activity for Monday morning and has no further expectations of effectiveness.

CRITERIA FOR SELECTION OF MATERIALS

Since there are no specific entities called "gifted materials," general criteria are offered for selecting materials appropriate for gifted students.

1. Materials should be geared to a reading level slightly above the student's present level of functioning.
2. Materials should stimulate small group discussion.
3. Materials should be diverse in respect to variety, point of view, and the integration of cognitive and affective components.
4. Materials should be geared to complex thought processes, especially the development of analytical skills.
5. Materials should be supplementary, rather than the substance of the program.

RESOURCES

Sources for curriculum materials for the gifted are varied. Here are some resource checkpoints.

1. Many excellent gifted curriculum materials can be discovered through an ERIC search initiated around specific topic areas. CEC Information Services can provide this search.
2. Curriculum bibliographies may be obtained from individual model programs throughout the country by contacting the program coordinator.
3. State Departments of Education develop good curriculum materials in gifted education. Write to the gifted state consultant for specific information.
4. Some packaged curriculum materials are excellent for use with gifted students, such as those listed in the following section. However, many materials now being sold commercially are, upon examination, of little help in building a sound program. Application of the criteria for selection of materials previously presented is a good test of their appropriateness.

SELECTED MATERIALS FOR GIFTED PROGRAMS

The following lists of materials are categorized by type. They have been field tested and found to be successful in specific gifted programs, based on the objectives of those programs. These lists are representative rather than exhaustive.

Mastery Level

CEMREL Math Program, CEMREL Labs, St. Louis MO (Grades 7–12)
Ginn Reading 720, Ginn & Co., 191 Spring St., Lexington MA 02173.
Introductory Physical Science (IPS) (Grades 7–8)
Junior Great Books, Junior Great Books Foundation, 400 Michigan Ave., Chicago IL (Grades 2–8)
Lipman, M. *Philosophy in the Classroom: A Guide for Teachers.* Upper Montclair NJ: Institute for the Advancement of Philosophy, 1976.
Lipman, M. *Philosophy for Children Series.* Upper Montclair NJ: Institute for the Advancement of Philosophy. Selected titles: *Harry Stottlemeier's Discovery* (rev. ed.), 1977; *Lisa,* 1977; *Suki,* 1978. (Student readings)

Critical Thinking Skills

Attribute Games and Activities, Creative Publications, 1101 Antonio Rd., Mountain View CA 94043
Basic Thinking Skills, Midwest Publications, P.O. Box 129, Troy MI 48099
Classroom Quickies: Books 1–3, Midwest Publications, P. O. Box 129, Troy MI 48099
Critical Thinking, Books 1–2, Midwest Publications, P.O. Box 129, Troy MI 48099
The First Thinking Box, Benefic Press, 10300 W. Roosevelt Rd., Westchester IL 60153
SRA Think Box, Science Research Associates, 1540 Page Mill Rd., Palo Alto CA 94304
Wordly Wise, Educators Publishing Service, 75 Moulton St., Cambridge MA 02138

Theoretical Models

SOI Learning Materials, SOI Institute, 214 Main St., El Segundo CA 90245
Thinking Caps, Box 7239, Phoenix AZ 85011
Williams, F. *Classroom Ideas for Encouraging Thinking and Feeling.* Buffalo NY: DOK Publishers, 1970.

Interdisciplinary

Bronowski, J. *Ascent of Man*. Boston: Little, Brown & Co., 1974.

Burke, J. *Connections*. Boston: Little, Brown & Co., 1978.

Clarke, D. (Ed.). *The Encyclopedia of How It Works*. New York: A & W Publishers, 1977.

Clarke, D. (Ed.). *The Encyclopedia of How It's Made*. New York: A & W Publishers, 1978.

Clarke, D. (Ed.). *The Encyclopedia of How It's Built*. New York: A & W Publishers, 1979.

Clarke, K. *Civilization*. New York: Harper & Row, 1969.

Man: A Course of Study. Curriculum Development Associates, 1211 Connecticut Ave., Suite 414, Washington DC 20036.

Keylin, A. (Ed.). *Science of the Times, 1-2*. New York: Times Books, 1977.

Toynbee, A. (Ed.). *Cities of Destiny*. New York: Weathervane Books, 1967.

Creative Thinking

Feldhusen, J. (Ed.). *The Purdue Creative Thinking Program*. West Lafayette IN: Purdue University, 1970.

The Five Sense Store: The Aesthetic Education Program, CEMREL Inc., Viking Press, and Lincoln Center for the Performing Arts, 625 Madison Ave., New York NY 10022.

Myers, R., & Torrance, E. P. *Ideabooks*. Lexington MA: Ginn & Co., 1965.

Renzulli, J. S. *New Directions in Creativity (Mark One, Mark Two, Mark Three)*. Evanston IL: Harper & Row, 1976.

Critical and Creative Thinking (Problem Solving)

The Productive Thinking Program, Charles E. Merrill Co., 1300 Alum Creek Dr., Columbus OH 43216

REFERENCES

Bloom, B. S. *Taxonomy of educational objectives: Cognitive and affective domains*. New York: Longman, 1969.

Feldhusen, J., & Kolloff. A three-stage model for gifted education. *G/C/T*, 1978, *1*, 53-58.

Guilford, J. P. *The nature of human intelligence*. New York: McGraw-Hill, 1967.

Meeker, M. *Structure of intellect: Its interpretation and uses*. Columbus OH: Charles E. Merrill, 1969.

Renzulli, J. S. *The enrichment triad model: A guide for developing defensible programs for the gifted and talented*. Wethersfield CT: Creative Learning Press, 1977.

Williams, F. *Classroom ideas for encouraging thinking and feeling*. Buffalo NY: DOK Publishers, 1970.

CHAPTER 11

Evaluation of Gifted Programs

JOYCE VAN TASSEL

Gifted program evaluation provides information useful in making decisions about the future of gifted programs at any particular period of time at local, state, and national levels. The term *evaluation* is defined as (1) an ascertainment of merit; or (2) a delineating, reporting out, or collecting of data for decision making purposes. If we apply this definition to gifted program evaluation, we are concerned first of all that the program show merit to its participants as well as its observers. Secondly, we are concerned that a defensible procedure be followed for setting up the evaluation design and gathering needed data. In terms of making decisions about gifted programs, most administrators are interested in addressing two major questions:

1. How effective are the processes by which the program was set up in terms of continuing the same program design for another year?
2. What has been the benefit of the program to the individual student and/or students as an aggregate?

PROGRAM DEVELOPMENT EVALUATION

Evaluation data help us assess the effectiveness of the program development steps followed in establishing the gifted program. Needs assessment must be conducted on at least an annual basis in order to ascertain properly whether or not both student needs and program needs are being met. The process of needs assessment itself, however, should be examined in light of evaluation data. Reasonable questions such as the following should be posed in order to determine the overall effectiveness of the needs assessment:

1. Are all the needs of gifted students being considered when planning the program?
2. Is program input being solicited from adequate numbers of people and publics?

Program goals, objectives, and activities should also be evaluated on an annual basis. During the course of a school year, it is not unusual for teachers to shift student objectives and activities in light of new information, their own particular constraints as teachers, or for other reasons. Such changes should be accounted for through a specific evaluation process that allows all who work in the program to understand the rationale behind them.

The staff development process also requires an annual evaluation. Not only should we look at the effectiveness of individual inservice programs conducted throughout a school year, but at the progress and sequential development achieved by participants in the staff development program as a whole. Those participants include teachers of the gifted, administrators, and others who come in contact with such workshops.

Curriculum development procedures and outcomes should also be evaluated. It is not enough to say that a group of teachers will develop a differentiated curriculum for gifted students at the sixth grade level. The processes and the products of such development must be carefully evaluated. It is not unusual for teachers to mistranslate gifted program models and make them something they were never intended to be. For example, the use of Bloom's taxonomy in a curriculum design does not automatically yield appropriate activities for the gifted unless the teachers constructing those activities can translate the steps of the model appropriately.

Perhaps the most important program development step requiring careful evaluation is the identification procedure by which a population is selected and targeted for programing. If this phase of program development is not evaluated it may very well spell the demise of the program itself. Questions such as the following need to be asked on an annual basis:

1. Are the most appropriate criteria being used for consideration of candidates for the program?

2. Are the cutoff points reasonable?

3. Are the specific instruments being used as valid and reliable as possible?

4. Is the overall identification process defensible?

STUDENT GROWTH EVALUATION

It has often been argued that gifted programs demonstrate little more than the fact that students enjoy them and that teachers are stimulated by the nature of the population they are working with. Unfortunately, in an age of accountability, this is insufficient documentation to justify gifted programs as beneficial to those for whom they were designed. Thorough evaluation evidence must be provided, documenting student growth on both cognitive and affective dimensions.

In order to gather such evidence we must carefully construct evaluation designs that are appropriate to the kinds of objectives and activities we are attempting to carry out with students. Toward that end, we need to examine pretest and posttest results on instruments that show cognitive growth, as well as pre- and postattitudinal scales that demonstrate affective growth. Figure 1 outlines appropriate evaluation methodology for each of three program approaches.

It is often difficult to demonstrate cognitive growth for gifted students because of the following constraints:

1. Many gifted programs do not run for more than 1 to 2 hours per week.

2. Posttesting cannot yield significant results because gifted students are already operating at the 95th to 99th percentile during pretesting for whatever area of giftedness they have been selected.

3. Adequate test measures do not exist that can measure discrepancy in gifted students' growth in a particular area.

4. The gifted program itself may not be the sole factor contributing to student growth. Many intervening variables, such as experience in the regular classroom and in the home, may be equally significant factors.

Although these constitute major obstacles, it is still important to attempt to assess growth that is believed to be a result of a specific program falling under the rubric of gifted education. Figures 2, 3, 4, and 5 represent specific examples of attempts to quantify and measure what occurs in a gifted program at each of four grade levels (K-3, 4-6, 7-8, and 9-12) and in three content areas (language arts, science, humanities).

Perhaps the most revolutionary approach to measuring student growth has been the use of off level testing, especially with aptitude instruments, for purposes of detecting discrepancies in growth from the entering date to the exiting date of the program. The work of Dr. Julian Stanley at Johns Hopkins University has led the way to wider usage of this particular technique. Collecting student growth data can also be done through proficiency

FIGURE 1
Evaluation Outcomes for Program Approaches

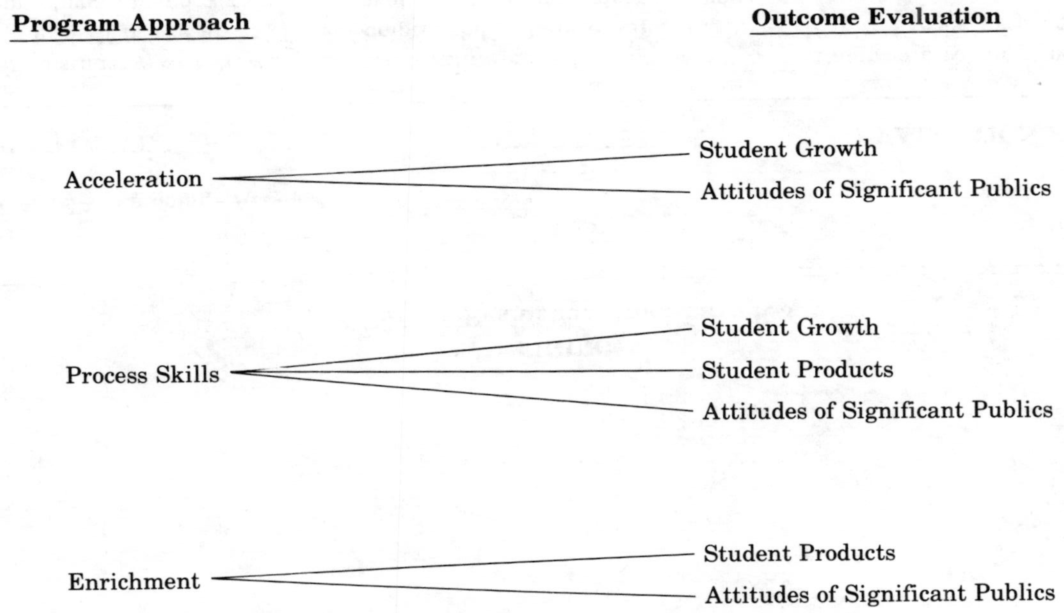

Program Approach

Outcome Evaluation

Acceleration
- Student Growth
- Attitudes of Significant Publics

Process Skills
- Student Growth
- Student Products
- Attitudes of Significant Publics

Enrichment
- Student Products
- Attitudes of Significant Publics

FIGURE 2
Sample Evaluation Procedures K-3

LEVEL: Grades K-3
CONTENT AREA: Language Arts

OBJECTIVES	ACTIVITIES	EVALUATION PROCEDURES
Identified gifted students will show at least 2 years growth in the areas of reading comprehension and vocabulary.	Students will: • Comprehend, analyze, and evaluate basal reading materials, Newberry Award books, and special interest materials. • Learn a minimum of 10 vocabulary words each week.	Diagnostic reading test (e.g., Gates McGinitie) to be used on a pretest/posttest basis.

	Students will:	
Identified gifted students will develop expository writing skills as measured by pretest and posttest writing samples.	• Be able to construct a paragraph in the form of topic sentence, attitude, support statements, and summary. • Write in class at least three times per week.	Pretest and posttest student writing sample based on the following criteria: • Structure • Grammar • Content • Vocabulary usage • Originality Samples will be evaluated by at least four people (e.g., three teachers, one administrator). 75% of the post samples will fall in the 4-5 range on a 5 point scale.
Identified gifted students will improve critical and creative thinking abilities by 30% on a pretest/posttest measure.	• Participate in small group discussions dealing with current events, special interest topics, and interpersonal relations via a structured discussion mode. • Practice critical thinking with mind benders and simple logic problems. • Develop skills in position supports, listening and response techniques, and topical fluency.	Pretest and posttest discussion tapes showing general improvement in critical and creative discourse. Tapes will be evaluated by at least three people. Pretest and posttest teacher-selected critical thinking problems of equal complexity. Pretesting and posttesting on the Torrance Tests of Creative Thinking, Verbal Forms (Activities 3 and 7)

FIGURE 3
Sample Evaluation Procedures 4-6

LEVEL: Grades 4-6
CONTENT AREA: Language Arts

OBJECTIVES	ACTIVITIES	EVALUATION PROCEDURES
Identified gifted students will increase language skills by two grades beyond placement.	Students will practice language development via the following: • Vocabulary builders • Crossword puzzles • Syntax problems • Study of Greek and Latin (prefixes and suffixes) • Root word activities • Classifying, analogies, synonyms, and antonyms.	Proficiency tests on grammar and vocabulary.

Objective	Activities	Evaluation
Identified gifted students will improve writing skills by at least two levels, based on pretest and posttest writing samples.	Students will: • Use the library and other resources such as interviews and field trips. • Practice in-class theme writing. • Work on mind benders and logic problems. • Participate in discussions and debates on controversial issues.	Pretesting and posttesting by writing themes on topics that have been researched, to be graded by the teacher and three other professionals through holistic grading using a criteria checklist. Students will improve by 2 points on 1 to 5 point system.
Identified gifted students will improve their abilities to think and read critically by 30% as a result of the program.	Students will: • Work on problem solving activities. • Develop analytical skills through selective reading and group discussion. • Practice verbal logic problems (analogies, syllogisms, etc.).	Pretesting and posttesting on the Watson Glaser Critical Thinking Appraisal. Teacher-made pretest/posttest reading samples to be analyzed by students.

FIGURE 4
Sample Evaluation Procedures 7-8

LEVEL: Grades 7-8
CONTENT AREA: Science

OBJECTIVES	ACTIVITIES	EVALUATION PROCEDURES
Identified gifted students will increase their skills in scientific experimentation at least two ranges in proficiency on a teacher made rating scale as judged by pretest and posttest experiments.	Gifted students will master the following: • Scientific terminology • The tools of the scientist • The process of experimentation	Pretest and posttest experiments judged for discrepancy on a 1 to 5 scale by a panel of science teachers not in the program.
Identified gifted students will produce a science project that receives a commendation level rating at the local science fair.	Gifted students will master the skills of research through: • Conducting mini-projects in class in pairs and writing conclusions. • Presenting at least one science experiment to the class, complete with charts and other necessary information.	Product rating scale completed by instructor. Rating assigned at science fair.
Identified gifted students will master basic statistical methods by scoring at 80% proficiency level on a posttest.	Gifted students will learn basic research design procedures and test for significant differences.	Teacher-made test on statistical methods.

FIGURE 5
Sample Evaluation Procedures 9-12

LEVEL: Grades 9-12
CONTENT AREA: Humanities

OBJECTIVES	ACTIVITIES	EVALUATION PROCEDURES
Identified gifted students will increase their ability to understand underlying forms and systems of knowledge by 50% on a pretest/posttest measure.	Students will be exposed to the underlying forms in art, music, literature, history, and philosophy through reading and doing group projects. Students will prepare class presentations on systems of knowledge in small groups.	Teacher-made pretests and posttests on forms and systems of knowledge.
Identified gifted students will demonstrate increased ability to integrate content areas as judged by an individual research project at a level 2 years beyond student placement.	Students will: • Develop a topic that spans at least three areas of the humanities. • Write and illustrate the topic. • Interview experts in each area.	Panel of experts (at least three) will assess the research projects on a rating scale according to predetermined criteria.
Identified gifted students will increase their understanding of human value systems as judged by pretest and posttest performance scores of at least 1 point difference on written essays.	Students will: • Study the lives of famous artists in each area of the humanities. • Study the cultural milieu of the artists. • Prepare an oral presentation on "Human Values of the Artist."	Teacher-constructed essay questions on a pretest/posttest basis as judged on a 1 to 5 rating scale.

tests within content areas, as well as through diagnostic tests that examine specific skills and abilities. The following list demonstrates types of tests and at least one example of each that have been utilized in gifted programs to show growth:

Achievement Tests (used at advanced levels for off level testing)
- California Test of Basic Skills
- Iowa Test of Basic Skills
- Metropolitan Achievement Tests
- Ross Cognitive Abilities Test

Aptitude Tests
- School College and Abilities Test (SCAT)
- Differential Aptitude Test (DAT)

Diagnostic Tests
- SOI Tests
- Learning Abilities Tests (all levels)
- Gates McGinitie (reading, elementary)
- Orleans-Hanna (math, grades 5-8)

Critical Thinking Tests
- Watson-Glaser Critical Thinking Appraisal (Grades 6-12)
- Cornell Critical Thinking Test (Grades 9-12)

Creativity Tests
- Torrance Tests of Creative Thinking, Verbal (2 forms)
- Torrance Tests of Creative Thinking, Figural (2 forms)

Proficiency Tests in New Areas of Exposure (e.g., foreign language)
- Algebra Cooperative Test
- High school exams administered at junior high level in appropriate content areas

Other approaches are also helpful to document student growth in certain kinds of programs where the collection of hard data is extremely difficult. These include directed observation; interviews (small group and individual); case conferences; checklists, inventories, questionnaires; rating scales; charts or graphs of pupil progress; logs or journals; autobiographies, diaries; samples of student work; tape recordings; and cumulative records.

PARTICIPANTS IN EVALUATION

For purposes of program growth and expansion, ensuring that sufficient numbers and types of publics have been asked to evaluate the program is a major consideration. At least *four* publics should be surveyed in any gifted program evaluation. Students, teachers, parents, and administrators all must be allowed to communicate their perceptions of the effect of the program on themselves and on the students who are participating in it.

Within each of these groups, it is important to have a sufficient and representative sample. Teachers who work with gifted students as well as those who do not should fill out questionnaires. Central office administrators as well as building administrators, such as principals, should likewise be assessed. In this manner, the gifted program coordinator can be assured of a representative picture regarding attitudes toward the program. Although the picture thus obtained may be more perceived than actual, it does provide needed data for the next steps in planning. Forms 1 and 2 may be useful for surveying students and parents, respectively.

WHAT ARE THE STEPS IN PROGRAM EVALUATION?

The three general steps of delineating, collecting, and reporting data can be broken down into five specific areas for purposes of planning an appropriate evaluation design. The evaluation design should be developed in conjunction with planning the objectives and mechanics of the gifted program. It is the planning document that sets forth the scope and sequence of the evaluation effort. A sound evaluation design should include the following components:

- *Performance Objectives:* Statements of expected program outcomes for students, parents, administrators, and staff. These should be stated in terms of the individual who will be exhibiting the behavior, the behavior itself, and the objective of the behavior.
- *Measurement Devices:* Names or descriptions of instruments to be used in measuring objectives.
- *Criterion Levels:* Statements of what level or degree of attainment of the objective indicates success.
- *Data Collection Schedule:* A timetable for administering the instruments and compiling the report.
- *Data Analysis Procedures:* How data is to be analyzed, such as adding totals, figuring percentages, computing means. Sophisticated statistical procedures are not likely to be necessary.

Forms 3 and 4 illustrate two separate types of objectives for a gifted program.

TIPS FOR CONDUCTING A SMOOTH EVALUATION

The process of conducting program evaluation can be both onerous and threatening if careful planning has not occurred. Early consideration of several important factors can reduce the burden of evaluation for everyone.

Timing of Data Collection

Try to select a time schedule which spaces activities throughout the program year. Two critical times to avoid are the beginning and ending weeks of school. Testing and other inventories can often be conducted during "off" time periods in regard to the program. A quick check with staff before the schedule is set can save time and eliminate bad feelings.

Standardization of Procedures

In order to obtain reliable data, instruments must be administered under similar conditions. Written instructions to teachers, even for attitudinal instruments, can be helpful in keeping procedures consistent. At least one staff development session at the beginning of the year should be devoted to a discussion of evaluation procedures.

Organization of Data in a Simplistic Manner

Remember that people who know little about gifted education will be perusing the data. Prepare the material as logically and consistently as possible. Include a table of contents and paragraph introductions that share the nature of the data and any valid interpretations that can be made.

Consistency in Format and Data Reporting

Charts or supporting graphs give the reader a quick overview of an evaluation report. Avoid long or complicated summary tables. Condense data so that the layman can interpret it easily.

Final Evaluation Report

Send the report to all evaluation participants as well as key decision makers within the school district. Ask for a slot on the school board calendar to share salient points. A good, interpretive summary of the data collected is invaluable and should precede the body of the report.

USE OF THE EVALUATION DATA FOR FUTURE PLANNING

Perhaps the most important use of evaluation data is for the purpose of future planning and decision making. The data gleaned should provide answers to the following critical questions:

1. Are the right students being selected for the program in the right numbers?
2. What aspects of the curriculum need revision?
3. Are activities of the program appropriate to the needs of the students?
4. Is the staff capable of carrying out the goals and objectives of the program?
5. Is the staff development component successful? How should it be structured next year?
6. Should the program continue in its present form with modifications, or should a new kind of program be instituted?

Decisions in each of these areas need to be made annually. Only sound evaluation data can facilitate intelligent decision making so that programs can be modified or expanded in ways that truly meet the needs of gifted students.

FORM 1
Student Questionnaire

	Yes	No
1. I asked to be in this class.		
2. I was chosen by the teacher(s) to be in this class.		
3. I find the work in this class a little too easy.		
4. The work in this class moves too slowly.		
5. In this class we can express ideas openly.		
6. I am better in this subject than in other subjects.		
7. I am given more responsibility for my own learning in this class than in my regular classes.		
8. In this class we can learn as much about the subject as we want to learn.		
9. In this class I can work at my own speed.		
10. In this class I understand why I did well or poorly.		

FORM 2
Parent Attitude Survey

We are anxious to determine the attitudes of parents toward our programs. Therefore, we have prepared the following set of questions. We hope you will take a few minutes to fill out this form and return it to the indicated address. Fifteen questions are listed. In the spaces provided at the right, you are asked to indicate the following:

Strongly Agree . . . . .SA
Agree . . . . A
Not Applicable . . . . NA
Disagree . . . . .D
Strongly Disagree . . . . .SD

Indicate only one check (✔) for each question. Please respond to each item. Space is provided for you to comment on each question, if you care to do so. Also, two additional questions are asked which require a written response. We would appreciate it if you would take the time to respond to these questions as well. You may use the back of the sheets if you need additional space.

	SA	A	NA	D	SD
1. This program meets the needs of my child. Comments:					
2. I feel that I understand what is taking place in the program. Comments:					
3. This program has had a positive influence on my child's attitude toward school. Comments:					

FORM 2 (continued)

	SA	A	NA	D	SD
4. This program has increased my child's self confidence. Comments:					
5. This program has enlarged my child's friendships. Comments:					
6. I do not feel that my child is missing the "basics" as a result of this program. Comments:					
7. I think this program should be continued. Comments:					
8. I think it is important to have my child work with children of similar academic ability. Comments:					
9. I am not concerned about my child being away from the regular classroom. Comments:					
10. I am pleased that this program lets students of similar academic interests and abilities work together. Comments:					

FORM 2 (continued)

	SA	A	NA	D	SD
11. I am pleased that this program uses my child's current interests to develop indepth academic activities. Comments:					
12. I am pleased that my child is able to develop new interests in this program. Comments:					
13. I am pleased that my child is exposed to areas of the curriculum in which he/she hasn't worked before. Comments:					
14. I am pleased that this program tries to develop greater enthusiasm in my child for academic pursuits. Comments:					
15. I am pleased that my child is able to bypass (avoid) repetitious and inappropriate requirements. Comments:					

A. What has been the most beneficial thing that has happened to your child as a result of participating in this program?

B. What suggestions would you have for improving the program?

FORM 3
Sample Evaluation Design for Student Growth

Objective Measurement	Seventh grade gifted students will demonstrate mastery of algebra and advanced algebra as measured by the Cooperative Algebra Tests.
Criterion Level	By the end of the school year, 90% of the students will have scored at least 35 out of 40 points on the Algebra I test, and at least 30 out of 40 points on the Algebra II test.
Data Collection Schedule	Pretest on Form A of Algebra I–September 3, 1981 Posttest on Form B of Algebra I–December 17, 1981 Pretest on Form A of Algebra II–January 3, 1982 Posttest on Form B of Algebra II– May 29, 1982 Data compiled for year by June 6, 1982 Report submitted by June 15, 1982
Data Analysis Procedures	In order to analyze this data, I will compute the percentage of students scoring at least 35 points on the Algebra I test. Then I will determine how many also scored at least 30 points on the posttest. If this percentage equals 90% or greater, I will have met my criterion for success.

FORM 4
Sample Evaluation Design for Parent Attitudes

Objective Measurement	Parents of students participating in the gifted program will demonstrate positive attitudes toward the quality of the gifted program as measured by a parent attitude questionnaire.
Criterion Level	Eighty percent of the parents will indicate a positive attitude as defined by a total score of +1 or greater on the instrument. (A minimum return rate of 30% will be deemed acceptable.)
Data Collection Schedule	Questionnaire will be developed and reproduced by October 30, 1981. Questionnaire will be mailed to all parents on April 2, 1982. Questionnaire will be returned by April 20, 1982. If returns are low, a second mailing will occur April 25, 1982. This questionnaire will be returned May 10, 1982. Data compiled by May 20, 1982. Report submitted to school board by June 4, 1982.
Data Analysis Procedures	First, I must document a return rate of 30% on the questionnaires. Then, in order to analyze them, I shall tally a positive or negative score for each questionnaire returned and then figure the percentage of questionnaires having positive scores. If 80% of these scores are positive, I will have met my criterion for success.

CHAPTER 12

Budgeting for a Gifted and Talented Program

WILLIAM G. VASSAR

Two basic perspectives provide a framework for discussion of the budget for a gifted and talented program. First, the budget should be viewed as an equal partner with the instructional components of the program. Second, budget considerations should be examined in light of the implications for the total budget involving all children and youth in the school district.

School boards, with administrative assistance, set priorities over periods of time for the educational expenditures to be made by the public for educational purposes. A poorly constructed singular budget item could well mean the defeat of a total budget for all children and youth. In developing a program for the gifted and talented, caution and care should be taken to make the budget component an interdependent part not only of programs for the gifted and talented but also of the overall budget presented to the school board.

THEORETICAL CONSIDERATIONS

Irrespective of the name, a budget is an instrument for putting purposes, policies, and programs into effect. The budget for a gifted and talented program represents the fiscal interpretation of the education program developed within the school district to meet the needs of these children and youth. Generally speaking, a budget defines a gifted and talented program for a given period of time to achieve established purposes. It includes an estimate of expenditures and proposed sources of local, federal, state, and/ or private financial support. The budget is also an outward manifestation of personnel policy, since a major portion of expenditures is devoted to instructional and ancillary personnel.

Too many times, school districts have failed to receive local, state, or federal funding because of the failure of the budget to reflect the educational policies of the district and, more specifically, the instructional plan to implement a program for the gifted and talented. Thoughtful consideration of the concept of budget as a schematic plan for crystallizing organizational policies, plans, and resources reveals its potential for appraising, initiating, adjusting, planning, integrating, and controlling policies and the educational program. Therefore, the budget should become an integral part of the overall plan to serve the gifted and talented in a given school district. It cannot be treated merely as an "add-on" to be developed after the instructional components have been identified.

From another perspective, in numerous instances the local, state, and federal sectors appropriate a set amount of funds. The total appropriated at any level directly indicates the limitations for educational programing to meet the needs of the gifted and talented. Although the program planning team may be more idealistic than practical, it should build in a contingency plan for reducing the cost of the program without seriously impairing its instructional aspects.

The costs of programs for the gifted and talented do exceed the regular per pupil cost in the school district. This observation is based on the assumption that such educational programs and ancillary services require excess cost expenditures beyond the regular per pupil cost. Provision of specially trained instructional personnel, additional student evaluations, added transportation, and special facilities, materials, and equipment all indicate increased expenditures to the local budget.

The reasonable and wise expenditure and management of fiscal resources in order to assure quality control of instructional programs for the gifted and talented is a crucial concept. It is far too easy to expend our energies in the instructional sense and lose sight of the fiscal sense. The procurement, planning, integration, and evaluation of each fiscal account should mirror the educational objectives of the instructional program.

There are three phases in preparing a budget for the administrative road it must travel in order to be approved for purposes of implementation. These include (1) determination of the special education program for the gifted and talented to be carried out over a certain period of time; (2) estimate of expenditures necessary to realize program goals and objectives; and (3) estimate of funds anticipated from public and private sources. It is difficult to defend a budget request professionally without justification based on sound educational goals and objectives. The budget must therefore be conceived as an interdependent component of the program for the gifted and talented and of the overall educational programs for all children and youth in the school district.

Everything we hope to achieve in the educational program for the gifted and talented has a price tag attached to it. This necessitates obtaining needed financial resources, as well as implementing careful management and control procedures following the procurement of funds from local, state, or federal sources. Obviously, without procurement of fiscal resources from one or a number of public or private agencies, there is little chance of developing a quality program. The following discussion addresses the various funding sources for gifted and talented programing.

STATE FUNDING

A number of school district policies suggest that the gifted and talented can be served within the regular classroom. This position usually adopts the premise that the district curriculum is adequate to meet the needs of all children and youth. Various states have found, however, that this is a very difficult way to meet the needs of the gifted and talented, and have moved toward a budgetary model that provides excess funding options to assist local districts in supporting the extra costs of implementing a program. In recent years, an increasing number of states have passed legislation allowing extra cost funding to local districts. Prominent among them are California, Connecticut, Florida, Georgia, North Carolina, and Pennsylvania.

Obviously, there is a direct correlation between state funding and the growth of local programs in these states. Most are funded under a special education model that places gifted and talented education within the total framework of exceptionality. The basic premise behind such legislative thrusts indicates a trend on the part of legislators in these states to address the educational and fiscal needs of the gifted and talented in the same manner as they do handicapped children and youth. Recent surveys by The Council for Exceptional Children (1978) and individual states such as Connecticut, Florida, and North Carolina indicate budgetary amounts at state levels increasing under this state legislative approach.

Reasonable funding to implement legislation to meet the needs of the gifted and talented is a key factor, regardless of the legislative models implemented in any state. President Johnson's 1968 White House Task Force on the Gifted and Talented and the Marland Report to the US Congress in 1972 both indicated that a state statute *with proper funding* was a basic component needed by any state desiring to move toward a heavy increase in programing for the gifted and talented at the school district level.

FEDERAL FUNDING

Much has been written in recent years regarding increased activity by the federal sector in the education of the gifted and talented. A greater awareness throughout the country of the needs of the gifted and talented is evident. Appropriations, however, have been relatively low. They have been limited to activities designed to increase awareness of needs, identify and assist in the budgeting of exemplary programs, train leadership personnel, and provide seed money to assist states in developing long range plans for the gifted and talented.

Federal funding is still in a stage of infancy. For example, Public Law 95-561, Title IX, Section 904 presently being implemented by the US Office of Education had an appropriation of 6.28 million dollars for fiscal year 1980. Of these funds, 75% are to be distributed to the 50 states and various territories. The proposed rules governing such federal funding make it quite difficult for any state to make a reasonable impact on meeting the needs of its gifted and talented youth. Recommended funding for fiscal year 1981 is indicated as remaining at the same level.

Beyond the specific funding for the gifted and talented under Title IX, a number of other federal funding sources can be tapped. A paramount source is Title IV-C of Public Law 95-561. Each state receives a specified allotment of funds from the federal sector to identify and fund selected educational programs of an exemplary and innovative nature. Federal guidelines under this specific source give priority to the gifted and talented for funding purposes, and a number of states make it a higher priority when funds reach the state level.

At this time, the trend in fiscal funding at the federal level seems to indicate a seeding action to assist states and school districts in initiating steps to bring about long range programing through state and local funds. Although there has been continuous activity by advocacy groups to increase federal funding for the gifted and talented, the basic model to serve such children and youth has not been designed and marketed for the Congress to fund throughout the country. Until a marketable model has been developed and funded, the federal sector will continue playing the role of "seeding the soil," with intensive funding being fertilized by state and local funds.

PRIVATE FOUNDATIONS

Sporadic efforts to enlist the interest of large and small private foundations in the education of the gifted and talented have been attempted. Over the past 20 years, however, little or no interest has been indicated by the major foundations in this special area of education. Some small foundations have been open to limited funding for special target groups among the gifted and talented. However, most private foundations are limited in where and whom they can serve by their boards and bylaws.

A number of local programs throughout the country have received funds from local or regional private foundations to assist them in programing for the gifted and talented. Many of the grants made by such foundations are of limited duration and for a specific purpose even though they are fully funded. Many foundations also have a matching funds requirement. For example, a prominent program in a Northeastern state received an $85,000 incentive grant, but had to match it with a like amount of funds from other sources.

Private foundations are certainly a potential source of funding for the education of the gifted and talented. However, one should know the location of such foundations, and their limitations in terms of time, funding, and human resources for long range planning for the gifted and talented. The provision of seed money to initiate programs indicates the trend that such limited funding has followed up to now.

BUSINESS AND INDUSTRY

Although business and industry does, to a reasonable degree, contribute human resources to assist the gifted and talented, very little budgetary assistance has been allocated to meet the needs of this group throughout the country. This sector may well be the greatest untapped fiscal resource. Apparently the public area of education has not yet discovered a creative way of approaching and marketing a plan for receiving considerable funding from this source.

Higher education and other public and private institutions in our society have found a number of ways of wooing funds from business and industry to meet the needs of children, youth, and adults. Institutions of higher learning often place business and industry leaders on their Boards of Trustees. Within a short period of time, needed facilities and equipment find their way to specific campuses.

Obviously, there must be many gifted and talented industrialists and business people who could be approached on behalf of a new generation of talent. Certainly it is time that the movement on behalf of gifted and talented children and youth begin to brainstorm the possibilities and potential for funding from the "captains of commerce" throughout the country.

LOCAL BUDGETARY NEEDS

What resources does the local school district need to design, develop, and implement an effective program for the gifted and talented from a budgetary viewpoint? Costs will differ from district to district depending upon such factors as the ability to pay, local resources, and the size of the school district. When a state develops legislation to fund gifted and talented programs at the local level, it takes into account (1) what the program will receive *above and beyond* the average per pupil cost of education for every child, and (2) what budgetary components will determine the excess cost for the special program.

Following is a consideration of the various budget components that directly affect the design, development, and implementation of a sound program for the gifted and talented, taking into account the degree of availability of state funds for implementation at the local level.

Instructional Personnel

This area of the budget may represent the largest expenditure of funds for a school district. Estimates in selected states indicate that from 80% to 90% of excess cost funds would be relegated to such personnel. Although instructional staff are carefully selected and specially trained, the "extra compensation factor" should be considered inappropriate. Because this type of staffing will, in itself, represent excess cost, it is politically unwise to request added compensation above and beyond the normal salary structure. Such budgetary behavior tends to widen the gap of communication and cooperation with regular classroom teachers.

Excess cost expenditure for an instructional teacher for the gifted and talented can be reasonably defended before the public and the Board of Education when the instructional person can be shown to offer programs, activities, and services clearly beyond those being provided in the regular classroom. A proposed instructional staff position may be more difficult to defend under the "special class concept," which is usually looked upon by Boards of Education as a design that could be developed by rearranging already existing staff within a school. It certainly deserves consideration from a budgetary point of view.

Ancillary Personnel

These staff are employed by the district to perform pupil personnel activities. They may include counselors, school psychologists, social workers, and instructional aides. Such staffing is an integral part of the team approach to meeting all the needs of the gifted and talented. Many programs have fallen by the wayside because the total program was predicated on the instructional staff. The counseling, psychological, and social needs of the child are as important as the "front line" instructional needs.

Although ancillary personnel are maintained for all children and youth in the school district, the program for the gifted and talented (or any other special program) will bring added demands for time in the areas of testing, counseling, and classroom assistance. Budgetary considerations should be taken into account to assure appropriate identification and placement, follow up diagnostic services, and annual reviews. Experience has shown that a much more effective program results from the contributions of instructional and ancillary personnel working with the regular classroom teachers who send their gifted and talented students to resource centers and other instructional settings.

Materials

Most educational materials existing on the commercial market today are appropriate for use with all students. This impression is substantiated by even a quick visit to any instructional methods display or fair. Since a special program's most important component is the provision of a differentiated and/or qualitatively differentiated curriculum with similar instructional strategies, materials expenditures for the gifted and talented should be extremely prudent. Materials appropriately used for all students are not the type of excess cost expenditures Boards of Education relish observing in a special budget for the gifted and talented.

Equipment

Budget expenditures in the area of equipment for gifted and talented programs should be minimal. Guidelines for the purchasing of equipment should be developed in order to separate the needs of the general educational program from those of the special programs. Basic facility equipment such as tables, desks, and chairs, as well as instructional equipment directly related to the differentiated educational program, are considered reasonable budget requests. The budget expenditure may be factored at a higher level for regional or cooperative programs for specific aptitude areas such as mathematics, science, or the arts.

Tuition

When the needs of gifted and talented children and youth cannot be met by the school district itself, other alternatives may need to be explored, taking into consideration the resources available outside the district. These resources may include (1) tuition to regional programs addressing specific aptitudes (Governor's School, Science Center, Arts Center, Marine Studies); (2) tuition to larger school districts that may be able to provide a program to gifted and talented youth from a smaller neighboring district; (3) tuition to colleges and universities to provide advanced educational programs for intellectually and artistically talented youth.

The cost effectiveness of the tuition approach should be closely monitored. Although tuition covers the educational costs of sending the gifted and talented to an alternative program, the district must consider added transportation costs as well.

Transportation

This budgetary line item reflects the design used in the educational program to bring the gifted and talented together for instructional purposes. If an itinerant teacher approach is used, this cost could represent the only professional transportation cost. In other instructional models, the gifted and talented may need to be transported to a cluster school certain days of the week.

School districts usually consider field trips *per se* a "red flag item" when they are listed solely for the gifted and talented. If it is necessary to transport students to special places for instructional purposes, the differentiated educational objective should reflect this need as it is related to the budget. School districts normally consider paying for only that transportation required beyond the normal transportation provided by the district. Travel by professional staff to workshops, conferences, or model programs should be included in this budget category.

Rental of Facilities

Space for providing the educational program for the gifted and talented may be limited or completely lacking. Renting outside facilities for such purposes is an alternative consideration. Decreasing school enrollments and school closings, however, have made this line item practically extinct in certain parts of the country.

Special Consultative Services

The school district may need to contract with others who are not employees of the district to provide special services for the gifted and talented. Such services may include (1) inservice programs to be conducted by college and university personnel; (2) outside evaluators to assist in the evaluation of the educational goals and objectives of the special program; (3) personal service contracts with artists or musicians who can provide special services not available from the regular school staff; (4) professionals to advise and assist in designing and developing a gifted and talented program for the school district.

COMPREHENSIVE BUDGETARY CRITERIA

Overall budgetary plans must be a reflection as well as an interdependent part of the total plan to meet the needs of the gifted and talented in a given school district. The following criteria should be applied as the budget is developed to assure that excellence is being attained.

An effective budget should:

1. Present a complete and all inclusive picture of the financial plan for the special program.
2. Consider the needs of all of the key components of the educational programs for the gifted and talented in relationship to each other and to the school district as a whole, articulation being a key factor.
3. Place responsibility for planning, preparing, and defending the budget with an administration directly responsible to the Board of Education.
4. Serve as an instrument of fiscal control to assure the school district and the community that expenditures are kept in line as projected in the total plan.
5. Demonstrate flexibility to assure the community that the needs of the gifted and talented are being met when emergencies necessitate changes from the original plan of operation.
6. Include adequate opportunities for informing the community of proposals contained in the plan for carrying out the educational components.

The budget component is essentially the fiscal translation of the educational components of the program for the gifted and talented. How it is interpreted to Boards of Education and the lay public may well determine how effectively the needs of the gifted and talented in any school district are met.

REFERENCE

The Council for Exceptional Children. *The nation's commitment to the education of gifted and talented children and youth: Summary of findings from a 1977 survey of states and territories.* Reston VA: The Council for Exceptional Children, 1978.

CHAPTER 13

Staffing in Relation to the Type of Personnel Needed

WILLIAM G. VASSAR

Staffing involves obtaining the best qualified professional and paraprofessional personnel to provide gifted and talented children and youth with quality instructional and ancillary services to nurture their unusual abilities. Staffing programs for the gifted and talented is an intricate and complex process due to the complicated mix of children and youth who are identified under a broadening concept of giftedness. The many types of giftedness uncovered in the past decade, coupled with the need for differentiation of instruction and development of materials, all contribute to the complexity of the staffing patterns emerging in the 1980's.

FACTORS AFFECTING STAFFING DECISIONS

Providing appropriate numbers and kinds of professional and paraprofessional staff to design, develop, and implement a total program of instruction and services for the gifted and talented is both significant and difficult. It is significant because the effectiveness of instruction and services rendered is directly influenced by the quality of administrative decisions made concerning staff size and competencies. It is difficult because of the variety of factors that enter into staffing decisions.

Staffing decisions are affected by a number of significant questions. For example, who are the gifted and talented? Which target groups of gifted and talented students will be served by the program? Why should they receive special treatment? What is the relationship between staffing for the gifted and talented and the total school staff? What types of differentiated

instruction and ancillary services will be offered? What teaching and counseling strategies should be used? What standards of competency should be
established? What administrative and supervisory needs exist? What are
the professional development needs of both the special and regular staff?

This chapter focuses on three groups of staff: instructional, ancillary, and
administrative or supervisory. These groups play the most important part
in planning for staffing, staff development, and delivery of quality services
and instruction to the gifted and talented in the school district. Although
personnel from the administrative and ancillary categories may not be as
visible as those who provide direct instruction, a total team effort is mandatory if a viable program of services is to be provided. The team concept
also promotes a full exploration of the broad questions previously posed
and helps to insure that the program itself will be articulated and coordinated with the total educational program of the school district.

PROGRAM PURPOSES

The goals and objectives of the instructional and ancillary program should
provide the focus for determining the nature and size of the staff selected,
as well as the scope of their activities. Certainly the abilities, skills, knowledge, and attitudes that the gifted and talented are expected to acquire
under the umbrella of staffing affects the size of the instructional staff.

The goals and objectives of the entire program for the gifted and talented
are the substance from which differentiated educational programs are de-
rived. For example, if the primary purpose of the program is to provide
differentiated instruction two days a week to the "intellectually gifted"
in grades four through six in a small suburban community, the number of
instructional and ancillary staff might be small and the need for administration rather limited. Selected goals determine the differentiated curriculum and instructional teaching strategies which the program provides and
affect the size of the staff necessary for their implementation.

SIZE AND SCOPE OF THE PROGRAM

The educational plan developed to meet the needs of the gifted and talented
greatly influences the size and composition of both the instructional and
noninstructional staff. This, in turn, conditions the kind and amount of
educational and ancillary services available to the gifted and talented. The
nature and extent of the special program to be implemented should be
designed against a background of existing plans, available facilities, community composition, social and educational change, and the fiscal realities
of funding and budgeting.

An overall needs assessment conducted with these factors in mind will
provide the administrator with an idea of the direction in which the com-

munity will move in terms of staffing. For example, if the budget is limited for staffing purposes, if the district is a rural setting with a small population, if the social and educational values of the community are conservative, and facilities are severely limited, the program staff may well consist of the regular classroom teacher given the benefit of inservice training on how to work with those with the greatest need in the regular class setting.

ORGANIZATION OF INSTRUCTION

The manner in which the gifted and talented are brought together to receive instructional or ancillary services also affects the size and composition of program staff. Any administrative plan to bring the gifted and talented together for such purposes should be developed in terms of educational objectives coupled with a sensitivity to community feelings relative to such issues as transportation and the complete separation of exceptional children and youth.

Throughout the history of the movement for gifted and talented youth in America, a number of plans have been implemented to assemble students for instructional purposes. These include separate classes, cross-graded groups, partial separation, adjunct programs (after school, Saturdays, or summer), honors groups, and independent study. Each of these designs reflects varying educational, social, and community viewpoints on reaching the educational objectives of the instructional programs for the gifted and talented.

Staffing patterns and the various administrative designs used to bring the gifted and talented together are closely interrelated. If the organizational design is to have significant impact upon educational programs, staffing considerations cannot be taken for granted. People, in the last analysis, are more important than structure.

GROUPING SIZE

The size of the group to be served by the program will have a profound and direct effect on the children and youth being served. Decisions on grouping size should therefore be considered in terms of the educational objectives of the program. Regardless of the design, each program needs a staff large enough to provide students with reasonable instructional and ancillary services to maximize their potential. The size of the group must take into consideration the amount of time students spend together, for what special purpose, and how many times a week they come together as a group or as individuals.

Since a variety of considerations affect the grouping size, it may be wise to examine two types of programs.

Type A: Special Class, Intellectually Gifted

This class is grouped for both general education and special education with one teacher for the entire day. The ideal standard enrollment is 15 pupils, but the most realistic is 18 to 20. The need for a counselor (10%) and a parttime school psychologist for testing (50%) should be considered.

Type B: Semi-Separation Program, Intellectually Gifted, Cross-Graded (Grades Four through Six)

This class meets the equivalent of one full day a week with a special teacher. Since the teacher may work with four different groups during the week, the daily group size is 10, but the teacher handles 40 different students per week. Students therefore spend 80% of their time in the regular classroom.

These examples are but two of the many variations of administrative designs to bring intellectually and artistically talented students together for instructional purposes. Each one must be weighed on an individual basis to determine optimum group size and teacher-pupil ratio. Three generalizations, however, can be offered.

1. Research studies favor smaller groupings.
2. Research does not point to any specific number of pupils as being optimum for all special education purposes.
3. Size should be planned in terms of educational objectives.

INSTRUCTIONAL STAFF

Characteristics

The instructional staff is composed of those professional and paraprofessional personnel who provide direct instructional services to many types of gifted and talented children and youth. Down through the decades and especially during the past few years, the literature has been loaded with "laundry lists" of desirable traits and characteristics of instructional staff who work with the gifted and talented. Gallagher (1975, p. 312) questioned the usefulness of such lists, stating that "anyone with an abundance of [the desirable] characteristics [generally quoted] ought to be able to achieve a position at the highest executive or professional level of our society."

Gold (1965, p. 419) commented, "What is needed is not the best teacher but the teacher who is best for working with a particular group of children; every child deserves such a teacher." At this time, when so many different target groups of gifted and talented students are being identified, those interested in the education of the gifted and talented may well have to consider more specific characteristics, personality traits, and competencies directly related to the type of gifted and talented children being served in a specific educational or alternative setting.

Gallagher (1975) addressed the total issue of characteristics best when he stated that we can no longer describe the gifted child by a general overall list of characteristics. Rather, it is essential to distinguish several subgroups of the gifted: the culturally different, the gifted underachievers, the creative, the talented, and the high performance gifted. Thus, we should be looking at specific personality traits, characteristics, and competencies as they relate to a specific target group of students. A general approach, by contrast, may well cloud the issue of identifying the best instructional staff for the gifted and talented.

Role of the Instructional Aide

As one continues to study the staffing of instructional programs for the gifted and talented, the role of the instructional aide should be considered. What type of person is needed to fill this role? What types of instructional assistance can this person provide? What types of educational requirements are desired?

Too often, the paraprofessional aide has not been screened and trained as thoroughly as aides or assistant teachers in general education and the education of the handicapped. This is an area of concern that should be addressed by the field through research in the coming years. More and more aides are being employed in programs for the gifted and talented with little consideration given to screening, abilities, skills, and need for training.

ANCILLARY STAFF

The instructional staff is only one part of the total staffing pattern that affects the educational, social, and emotional growth of the gifted and talented. Ancillary personnel are also of vital importance. They include those persons who render services which may or may not be directly related to the instructional process, and are comprised of pupil personnel specialists such as counselors, psychologists, social workers, and curriculum specialists. Representatives of the community and parents should also be taken into consideration.

There is a profound need for a team approach to the complete education of the gifted and talented. With an expanding concept of giftedness, the inclusion of pupil personnel specialists as part of that team, from the initiation of the program through its implementation, is especially critical. The direct involvement of central office and building level administration also helps to insure a true team approach to meeting the needs of the gifted and talented.

Although the literature abounds with information focusing on the importance of the instructional staff, both pupil personnel and administrative staff can contribute significantly to the success of a well rounded program for each and every gifted and talented child. The inclusion of administrative staff insures a communication line with the central office and the Board of Education, while the pupil personnel staff insures a planned diagnostic approach while screening and identification are taking place.

STAFFING—A TEAM APPROACH

A Planning and Placement Team (PPT) is delegated the responsibility by the superintendent of schools to screen, identify, and plan programs and services for the gifted and talented. This team is charged with carrying out the total program for the gifted and talented in the school district, with a direct line of responsibility to the central office. Each team should include administrators, instructional staff, pupil personnel specialists, curriculum specialists, and others who can contribute to the welfare of the gifted and talented. Parents should be actively involved in PPT activities as partners rather than mere observers.

Among the functions of the Planning and Placement Team are the overseeing of requests for service and programing, monitoring the referral process itself, the implementation of interim support procedures, and the formulation and subsequent evaluation of formal programs for the gifted and talented. With regard to interim support procedures, students identified as gifted and talented are at times assigned to a specialist or pupil personnel team for further study. During this exploratory time, there must be written documentation of alternative strategies initiated within the regular education program to serve these students. Too many times, a void in instructional programs or services exists before the student is placed in a program to meet his or her individual needs. This void can be eliminated by the use of the alternative strategies approach.

The following outline describes how the PPT functions within a school district and outlines each phase or level of the team's responsibilities.

Procedural Process for Screening and Identification

I. Request for Service and Programing
   A. Referral for Review Requested by
      1. Parent
      2. Teacher
      3. Administrator
      4. Any other individual knowledgeable about the child
   B. Reason for Referral
      1. Very high achievement

        2. High creative production

        3. Outstanding ability in the arts

        4. High test scores coupled with low achievement

        5. Task commitment

        6. Potential for achievement

    C. Referral Process

        1. Completed form requesting services submitted to PPT

        2. PPT coordinator assumes responsibility to

            a. Maintain log of referrals submitted

            b. Determine that parents have been informed

            c. Determine that all cumulative and relevant records have been reviewed

            d. Determine that all pertinent information has been gathered

            e. Determine disposition of referral

                i. Referral withdrawn by mutual consent if a preliminary check indicates that need has been met

                ii. Referral assigned to a specialist if concerns appear limited to a specific area

                iii. Referral scheduled for a Referral PPT meeting if formal screening and identification are indicated

II. Planning and Placement Team—Interim Period

    A. Initial Functions

        1. Gather and review all available data (records, tests, observations)

        2. Identify areas of demonstrated or potential giftedness and talent

        3. Examine current educational program to determine appropriate interim instructional strategies and program modification to be provided by regular classroom personnel

        4. Select alternative strategies for interim personnel, such as changes in instruction, classroom management techniques, supplemental academic or artistic instruction

        5. Implement and evaluate alternative strategies

    B. Evaluation Functions

        1. Evaluate effect of alternative strategies

        2. Evaluate all data gathered

        3. Determine whether special setting is needed or whether alternative strategies are meeting the instructional, social, and emotional needs of the student

III. Planning and Placement Team—Formal Structure

    A. Responsibilities

        1. Obtain comprehensive diagnostic study data necessary to determine special needs

2. Determine the student's eligibility for a differentiated program and related services
3. Formulate adequate and appropriate program
4. Recommend administrative design (resource room, special class, etc.)
5. Monitor and review design and program
6. Modify instructional program as appropriate

B. Membership
   1. Permanent members
      a. Administrative staff
      b. Pupil personnel staff
      c. Instructional staff

   2. Changing members
      a. Individual students
      b. Parents
      c. Regular or special program teachers

   3. Consulting members
      a. Experienced lay or professional persons warranted when a justifiable need exists for their instructional or diagnostic expertise

C. Roles of PPT Members
   1. Coordinator
      a. Schedule and conduct meetings with appropriate personnel
      b. Assure implementation of PPT recommendations
      c. Coordinate review functions of team

   2. Pupil personnel specialist
      a. Recommend types of identification and evaluation data needed
      b. Administer necessary testing
      c. Report all findings in written form
      d. Present findings and recommendations to team
      e. Assist in implementation of recommendations

   3. Regular classroom teacher
      a. Summarize reason for referral and previous alternative strategies used with the student
      b. Present other relevant data to PPT

   4. Parents
      a. Provide relevant information about child to PPT
      b. Attend PPT meeting and participate in discussions and decisions
      c. Give written consent for special program placement

5. Student
   a. Provide information to PPT by discussing personal perceptions of his or her special educational needs

D. Types of PPT Meetings
  1. Referral meeting
    a. Convene when informal alternative strategy has failed to meet individual student's needs
    b. Gather further data needed to implement special program

  2. Program meeting
    a. Review all data gathered from team members and other sources
    b. Determine feasibility of special program
    c. Recommend differentiated instructional program
    d. Set goals and objectives for both instructional and ancillary services

  3. Review meeting
    a. Convene at least annually
    b. Determine whether needs have been met
    c. Determine whether program needs modification
    d. Determine whether program should be continued and for what specific length of time

CONCLUSION

Many variables and complexities operate in relation to the staffing patterns a school district designs to meet the needs of the gifted and talented. The size of the district may sometimes limit the team approach when a small district lacks ancillary staff, or when a large district finds that the team approach becomes a maze of meetings. Administrators charged with program planning must therefore be aware of available human resources and the skills and competencies they have or lack, as well as long range goals and objectives for gifted and talented students and for all students in the district. They must then make prudent decisions on which program approach to adopt and the number and type of instructional and ancillary staff that can be assigned to carry out a reasonable differentiated program for the gifted and talented.

Staff planning is indispensible to the effective and economic operation of a program for the gifted and talented. An effective program maintains constant surveillance of staffing plans and policies in relation to an acceptable level of services designed to meet the educational objectives of the gifted and talented program.

Staffing decisions at the policy making level will be made in an environment of educational needs and the political realities of budgets and community values. Above all, those planning for the staffing of a program must view staffing as an interdependent part of both the gifted and talented program and the total education program of the district.

REFERENCES

Gallagher, J. J. *Teaching the gifted child* (2nd ed.). Boston: Allyn & Bacon, 1975.

Gold, M. *Education of the intellectually gifted.* Columbus OH: Charles E. Merrill, 1965.

CHAPTER 14

Resources

BOOKS

Abelson, H., & DiSessa, A. *Student science training program in mathematics, physics, and computer science.* Boston: Massachusetts Institute of Technology, 1976.

Abeson, A. R., Bolick, N., & Hass, J. *A primer on due process: Education decisions for handicapped children.* Reston VA: The Council for Exceptional Children, 1975.

Above and beyond: A teacher selected bibliography of instructional materials for use with gifted and talented students. Montgomery County Public School System, 1978.

Baker, H. J. *Biographical sagas of willpower.* New York: Vantage Press, 1970.

Baldwin, A. Y., Gear, G. H., & Lucito, L. J. *Educational planning for the gifted.* Reston VA: The Council for Exceptional Children, 1978.

Barr, R., et al. *Qualitatively differentiated programs for the gifted: Dade County USA responds.* Miami: Dade County Public Schools, 1978.

Bernstein, C. D., Hartman, W. T., Kirst, M. W., & Marshall, R. S. *Financing educational services for the handicapped.* Reston VA: The Council for Exceptional Children, 1976.

Boston, B. O. *Gifted and talented: Developing elementary and secondary school programs.* Reston VA: The Council for Exceptional Children, 1975.

Bransford, L. A., Baca, L., & Lane, K. *Cultural diversity and the exceptional child.* Reston VA: The Council for Exceptional Children, 1974.

Breiter, J. *Survey: Teachers of gifted elementary students.* Ames: Iowa State University, Elementary Education Office, 1979.

Brown, H. M. *A teacher education curriculum for gifted education.* Nashville TN: George Peabody College for Teachers, 1978.

Brumbaugh, F., & Pioscho, B. *Your gifted child: A guide to parents.* New York: Holt, 1959.

Cansler, D. P. *Programs for parents of preschoolers and parent group activities designed to broaden the horizons of young children.* Chapel Hill NC: Chapel Hill Training-Outreach Project, 1978.

Chambers, J. A., & Barron, F. *Identifying the culturally different gifted student.* Fresno: California State University, California State Education Department, 1978.

Clark, B. *Growing up gifted: Developing the potential of children at home and at school.* Columbus OH: Charles E. Merrill, 1979.

Cobb, S. G., et al. *Conn-Cept III. Once upon a building: Creating a differentiated learning environment for the gifted and talented.* Hartford: Connecticut State Education Department, 1978.

Coffy, K., et al. *Parents speak on gifted and talented children.* Ventura CA: Office of the Ventura County Superintendent of Schools, 1976.

Correll, M. M. *Teaching the gifted and talented, fast back 119.* Bloomington IN: Phi Delta Kappa Education Foundation, 1978.

The Council for Exceptional Children. *The nation's commitment to the education of gifted and talented children and youth.* Reston VA: The Council for Exceptional Children, 1978.

Edwards, J. D. *Effects of suggestive-accelerative learning and teaching (SALT) on creativity.* Ann Arbor MI: University Microfilms International, 1978. (Catalogue No. 7814940)

Evaluation of the exceptional child program for the gifted, 1975–76. Miami: Dade County Public Schools, 1976.

Feldhusen, J., & Treffinger, D. *Teaching creative thinking and problem solving.* Dubuque IA: Kendall/Hunt, 1977.

Fisher, E. *Investigation into the effects of positive labeling on the families of gifted children.* Ann Arbor MI: University Microfilms International, 1978. (Catalogue No. 7822045)

Fliegler, L. (Ed.). *Curriculum planning for the gifted.* Englewood Cliffs NJ: Prentice-Hall, 1961.

Fortna, R. O., & Boston, B. O. *Testing the gifted child: An interpretation in lay language.* Reston VA: The Council for Exceptional Children, 1976.

Fowler, E. C. *Study interrelating situational problem solving, math model building, and divergent thinking among gifted secondary mathematics students.* Ann Arbor MI: University Microfilms International, 1978. (Catalogue No. 7817574)

Glenn, P. G. *Relationship of self-concept and IQ to gifted students' expressed need for structure.* Atlanta: Georgia State University, 1978.

Goldman, N. T. *Gifted/talented curriculum bulletin no. 2: Differentiating.* New York: Community School District No. 4, 1977.

Griffin, D., & Plamondon, S. *Role of parents in a program for the gifted.* Richmond County GA: Association of the Gifted, 1978.

Grossi, J. A. *Model state policy, legislation and state plan toward the education of gifted and talented children and youth.* Reston VA: The Council for Exceptional Children, 1980.

Grost, A. *Genius in residence.* Englewood Cliffs NJ: Prentice-Hall, 1970.

Guidelines for the identification of the gifted and talented. Albany: New York State Education Department, 1977. (ERIC Document Reproduction Service No. ED 165 431.)

Hale, G. (Ed.). *The source book for the disabled.* London: Imprint Books, 1979. (Distributed in the US by Grosset & Dunlap)

Hebeler, J. R., & Reynolds, M. C. *Guidelines for personnel in the education of exceptional children.* Reston VA: The Council for Exceptional Children, 1976.

Higgins, S. T. *Special education administrative policies manual.* Reston VA: The Council for Exceptional Children, 1977.

Karnes, F. A., & Collins, E. C. *Handbook of instructional resources and references for teaching the gifted.* Boston: Allyn & Bacon, 1980.

Karnes, M. B. *Identifying and programming young gifted/talented handicapped children.* Urbana, Illinois: The Council for Exceptional Children, Illinois University, 1978.

Kaufman, F. *Your gifted child and you.* Reston VA: The Council for Exceptional Children, 1976.

Khatena, J. *Creatively gifted child: Suggestions for parents and teachers.* New York: Vantage Press, 1978.

Kroth, R. L., & Scholl, G. T. *Getting schools involved with parents.* Reston VA: The Council for Exceptional Children, 1978.

Kysilka, M. L., et al. *Preliminary study to determine the validity of the Annehurst curriculum.* Orlando: Central Florida University, 1979.

Lacy, G. *Suggested procedures for the identification of the gifted and talented.* Albany: New York State Education Department, 1978.

Lovitt, T. C. *Managing inappropriate behaviors in the classroom.* Reston VA: The Council for Exceptional Children, 1978.

Maker, C. J. *Providing programs for the gifted handicapped.* Reston VA: The Council for Exceptional Children, 1977.

Maker, C. J. *Training teachers for the gifted and talented: A comparison of models.* Reston VA: The Council for Exceptional Children, 1975.

Mandelbaum, J. *Study of the relationship of an inservice program in music and movement to opportunities for creativity in selected kindergartens.* Ann Arbor MI: University Microfilms International, 1978. (Catalogue No. 7824095)

Manning, D. *Toward a humanistic curriculum*. New York: Harper & Row, 1971.

Martinson, R. A. *Curriculum enrichment for the gifted in primary grades*. Englewood Cliffs NJ: Prentice-Hall, 1968.

Martinson, R. A. *Guide toward better teaching for the gifted*. National/State LTI for the Gifted and Talented, 1976.

Martinson, R. A. *The identification of the gifted and talented*. Reston VA: The Council for Exceptional Children, 1975.

Martorella, P. H. *Concept learning: Designs for instruction*. Scranton PA: Intext Education Publishers, 1972.

McCabe, M. V. *A matrix based plan to help identify gifted students*. Charlottesville: University of Virginia, 1978. (ERIC Document Reproduction Service No. ED 155 868.)

Meeker, M. N. *The structure of intellect: Its interpretation and uses*. Columbus OH: Charles E. Merrill, 1969.

Morra, F., Jr., & Hills, R. *Evaluation of the Alexandria, Virginia program for talented elementary students, 1974–1977*. Washington DC: Frank Morra & Associates, 1978.

Pal, H. I. *Child-rearing practices and locus of control in gifted adolescents*. Ottawa: National Library of Canada, 1977.

Perlini, E. L. *Developing a schoolwide enrichment activity program for identified gifted students*. Ft. Lauderdale FL: Nova University, 1978.

Renzulli, J. S., & Smith, L. H. *Guidebook for developing individualized exceptional programs (IEP) for gifted and talented students*. Mansfield Center CT: Creative Learning Publishers, 1979.

Reynolds, M. C., & Birch, J. W. *Teaching exceptional children in all America's schools—A first course for teachers and principals*. Reston VA: The Council for Exceptional Children, 1977.

Rinehart, B. C. *An inservice training program for elementary school teachers in reading instruction for the gifted and creative student*. Ann Arbor MI: University Microfilms International, 1978. (Catalogue No. 7814630.)

Robinson, H. B., et al. *Identification and nurturance of extraordinarily precocious young children: Annual report*. Chicago: Spencer Foundation, 1977.

Schurr, S. *Use a building learning center enrichment program to monitor needs of gifted/talented*. Bloomfield Hills MI: Vaughan Elementary School, 1979.

Shelby, M. E. *Who should teach the gifted?* Union TN: Council for the Exceptional Children (Primary/Intermediate Gifted Program), 1978.

Staff Handbook: MGM Pasadena Program. Pasadena CA: Pasadena Unified School District, 1977.

State plan for providing appropriate educational opportunities for the gifted and talented. Honolulu: Hawaii State Department of Education, 1977.

Storlic, T. R., et al. *Development of a culturally fair model for the early identification and selection of gifted children.* Educational Testing Services, Midwest Regional Office, 1978.

Strang, R. *Helping your gifted child.* New York: E. P. Dutton, 1960.

Strategies for site evaluation of gifted programs. San Diego CA: San Diego City Unified School District 92103, 1976.

Syphers, D. *Gifted and talented children: Practical programming for teachers and principals.* Reston VA: The Council for Exceptional Children, 1972.

Taubin, S., & Kane, N. *Sex education of the gifted and talented.* Philadelphia: Drexel University, 1978.

Tempest, N. R. *Teaching clever children: 7–11.* Boston: Routledge & Kegan Paul, Ltd., 1977.

Torrance, E. P. *Discovery and nurturance of giftedness in the culturally different.* Reston VA: The Council for Exceptional Children, 1977.

Tuttle, F. B., & Becker, L. A. *Characteristics and identification of gifted and talented students.* Washington DC: National Education Association, 1980.

Walker, V. *Teaching gifted children mathematics in grades 1–3.* Sacramento, California, 1973.

Weiner, B. B. (Ed.). *Periscope: Views of the individualized education program.* Reston VA: The Council for Exceptional Children, 1978.

Weintraub, F. J., Abeson, A. R., Ballard, J., & Lavor, M. L. (Eds.). *Public policy and the education of exceptional children.* Reston VA: The Council for Exceptional Children, 1976.

White, A. *Project SEARCH: Phase II evaluation.* (Describes development of procedures for assessing creative potential of handicapped children.) ERIC Document Reproduction Service No. ED 140 560.

White, A. J. *Conn-Cept VI: A primer on progressive development for the gifted/talented.* Hartford: Connecticut State Department of Education, 1978.

White, A. J., et al. *Conn-Cept VII: Task force report on curriculum, a primer on progressive development for the gifted and talented.* Hartford: Connecticut State Department of Education, 1978.

Whitmore, J. *Identifying and programming for highly gifted underachievers in the elementary school.* Paper presented at the 2nd World Conference on Gifted and Talented, San Francisco, 1977.

Williams, F. *Classroom ideas for encouraging thinking and feeling.* Buffalo: D.O.K. Publishers, 1970.

ARTICLES

Albert, R. S. Observations and suggestions regarding giftedness, familial influence and the achievement of eminence. *Gifted Child Quarterly,* 1978, *22* (2), 201.

Barbe, W. Pleasure or pain in the gifted child's family. *G/C/T,* 1978, *1* (1), 2.

Beebe, R. L. Creative writing and the young gifted child. *Roeper Review,* *1979, 1* (4), 27.

Bernstein, D. Critical thinking: An issue-oriented approach. *Roeper Review,* 1979, *1* (4), 8.

Biersdorf, M. P. Further adventures in language arts. *Roeper Review,* 1979, *1* (4), 19.

Blacher-Dixon, J., & Turnbull, A. P. A preschool program for gifted handicapped children. *Journal for the Education of the Gifted,* 1978, *1* (2), 15–23.

Blanning, J. Independent study and seminar program for urban gifted youth. *Roeper Review,* 1979, *1* (1), 15.

Boothby, P. Tips for teaching creative and critical reading. *Roeper Review,* 1979, *1* (4), 24.

Borland, J. Teacher identification of the gifted: A new look. *Journal for the Education of the Gifted,* 1978, *2* (1), 22.

Bruch, C. B. Recent insights on the culturally different gifted. *Gifted Child Quarterly,* 1978, *22* (3), 374.

Bruch, C. B., & Curry, J. A. Personal learnings: A current synthesis on the culturally different gifted. *Gifted Child Quarterly,* 1978, *22* (3), 313.

Burge, S. Rainy day–sunny day activities for gifted/creative/talented kids. *G/C/T,* 1979, *1* (1), 45.

Carroll, J. L. Creativity as an academic subject. *Creative Child and Adult Quarterly,* 1978, *3* (3), 161.

Chambers, J. A., & Barron, F. Culturally different gifted students: Identifying the ablest. *Journal of Creative Behavior,* 1978, *12* (1), 72.

Chisholm, S. Culturally disadvantaged gifted youth. *G/C/T,* 1978, *1* (5), 2.

Cleveland, M. E. Creative music strategies based upon poetry and the language. *Journal for the Education of the Gifted,* 1978, *1* (1), 29.

Cunningham, C. H., et al. Use of S.O.I. abilities for prediction. *Gifted Child Quarterly,* 1978, *22* (4), 506.

Dawkins, B. J. Do gifted junior high school students need reading instruction? *Journal for the Education of the Gifted,* 1978, *2* (1), 3.

Eason, B. L., & Smith, T. L. Perceptual motor programs for the gifted-handicapped. *Journal for the Education of the Gifted,* 1978, *2* (1), 10–21.

Elkind, J. The gifted child with learning disabilities. *Gifted Child Quarterly,* 1973, *17* (2), 96–7, 115.

Exum, H. A., & Colangelo, N. Enhancing self-concept with gifted black students. *Roeper Review,* 1979, *1* (3), 5.

Filstrup, J. M. Early development of a gifted young artist. *Gifted Child Quarterly,* 1978, *22* (4), 478.

Ford, B. G. Real help for the gifted physically handicapped: Barrier-free education. *Journal for the Education of the Gifted,* 1978, *1* (1), 25–28.

Ford, B. Student attitudes toward special programming and identification. *Gifted Child Quarterly,* 1978, *22* (4), 489.

Gallagher, P. A. Procedures for developing creativity in emotionally disturbed children. *Focus on Exceptional Children,* November 1972, *4,* 1–9.

Gay, J. E. Proposed plan for identifying black gifted children. *Gifted Child Quarterly,* 1978, *22* (3), 353–360.

Gear, G. Teachers of the gifted: A student's perspective. *Roeper Review,* 1979, *1* (3), 18.

Ginsberg, G. How to be a gifted parent in school. *G/C/T,* 1978, *1* (4), 37.

Gonzalez, G. Language, culture, and exceptional children. *Exceptional Children,* 1974, *40,* 565–70.

Gresson, A. D., & Carter, D. G., Sr. Equal educational opportunity for the gifted: In search of a legal standard. *Nolpe School Law Journal,* 1976, *6* (2), 145.

Grossi, J. A. *Gifted handicapped children.* Fact Sheet. Reston VA: The Council for Exceptional Children, 19.

Guy, M. What gifted education tests do colleges use? *Journal for the Education of the Gifted,* 1978, *2* (2), 94.

Hershey, M. Toward a theory of teacher education for the gifted and talented. *Roeper Review,* 1979, *1* (3), 12.

Hershey, M., & Kearns, P. Effect of guided fantasy on the creative thinking and writing ability of gifted students. *Gifted Child Quarterly,* 1979, *23* (1), 71.

Jacobs, J. C. Teacher attitudes toward gifted children. *Gifted Child Quarterly,* 1972, *16,* 23–26.

Jensen, S. Reading program for gifted high school students. *Roeper Review,* 1979, *1* (4), 25.

Karnes, F. A., & Collins, E. C. Close encounters of the productive kind: Community resources and the gifted/creative/talented. *G/C/T,* 1978, *1* (5), 38.

Karnes, F. A., & Collins, E. C. State definitions on the gifted and talented: A report and analysis. *Journal for the Education of the Gifted,* 1978, *1* (1), 44.

Kester, E. S. Gifted and basic education: Literary craft-tracking. *Creative Child and Adult Quarterly,* 1978, *3* (4), 215.

Khatena, J. Identification and stimulation of creative imagination imagery. *Journal of Creative Behavior,* 1978, *12* (1), 30.

Krawchuk, J. S. Library enrichment for the gifted. *Early Years,* 1978, *9,* (3), 30.

Lebeaj, M. Leadership and the law. *Roeper Review,* 1978, *1* (1), 19.

Le Rose, B. Quota system for gifted minority children: A viable solution. *Gifted Child Quarterly,* 1978, *22* (3), 394.

Levison, M. E. Emperor's new suite, or the scientific method exposed. *Journal of Creative Behavior,* 1978, *12* (2), 98.

Lewis, C. L., & Kanes, L. G. Gifted IEPs: Impact of expectations and perspectives. *Journal for the Education of the Gifted,* 1979, *2* (2), 61.

Maker, C. J. Searching for giftedness and talent in children with handicaps. *The School Psychology Digest,* 1976, *5,* 24–36.

Meeker, M. Developing a model for career guidance for the gifted. *Roeper Review,* 1978, *1* (2), 23.

Meeker, M. Measuring creativity from the child's point of view. *Journal of Creative Behavior,* 1978, *12* (1), 52.

Meisgeier, C., & Werblo, D. Factors compounding the handicapping of some gifted children. *Gifted Child Quarterly,* 1978, *22* (3), 325–331.

Mitchell, P. B., & Erickson, D. K. Education of gifted and talented children: A status report. *Exceptional Children,* 1978, *45* (1), 12.

Ng, Jolson. Using an old thing to teach the new stuff. *Roeper Review,* 1978, *1* (2), 23.

Norton, K. Teaching cooking as an alternative to force-feeding facts. *Journal for the Education of the Gifted,* 1978, *2* (2), 106.

O'Neill, K. K. Parent involvement: A key to the education of gifted children. *Gifted Child Quarterly,* 1978, *22* (2), 235.

Open letter to School District "X" from a disillusioned parent. *G/C/T,* 1978, *1* (4), 23.

The parent-professional partnership. Special issue of *Exceptional Children,* 1975, *41* (8).

Petrosko, J. M. Measuring creativity in elementary schools: The current state of the art. *Journal of Creative Behavior,* 1978, *12* (2), 109.

Plowman, P. D. Training teachers. *Roeper Review,* 1979, *1* (3), 14.

Progress by partners in step. Special issue on the IEP. *Teaching Exceptional Children,* 1978, *10* (3).

Renzulli, J. S. Talent potential in minority group students. *Exceptional Children,* 1973, *39* (6), 437–444.

Rivlin, H. How can we teach the gifted and talented we do not reach? *Roeper Publications,* 1978, *12* (3), 6.

Schauer, G. H. Emotional disturbance and giftedness. *Gifted Child Quarterly,* 1976, *20* (4), 470–477.

Silver, R. What is good teaching for the gifted? *Roeper Publications,* 1978, *12* (3), 12.

Smilansky, M. Culturally disadvantaged gifted youth. *G/C/T,* 1978, *1* (5), 3.

Stanley, J. Educational non-acceleration: An international tragedy. *G/C/T,* 1978, *1* (3), 2.

Swenson, E. V. Teacher-assessment of creative behavior in disadvantaged children. *Gifted Child Quarterly,* 1978, *22* (3), 338.

Tittle, B. Searching for hidden treasure: Seeking the culturally different gifted child. *Journal for the Education of the Gifted,* 1979, *2* (2), 80.

Torrance, E. P., & Torrance, J. P. Developing creativity instructional materials according to the Osborn-Parnes creative problems solving model. *Creative Child and Adult Quarterly,* 1978, *3* (2), 80.

Trezise, R. L. What about a reading program for the gifted? *Reading Teacher,* 1978, *31* (7), 742.

Vida, L. Children's literature for the gifted elementary school child. *Roeper Review,* 1979, *1* (4), 22.

Vining, P. F. Literature 001: A minicourse for the young gifted child (K-3). *G/C/T,* 1978, *1* (4), 40.

Williams, A. Teaching gifted students how to deal with stress. *Gifted Child Quarterly,* 1979, *23* (1), 136.

Witty, E. P. Equal educational opportunity for gifted minority group children: Promise or possibility? *Gifted Child Quarterly,* 1978, *22* (3), 344.

Wooster, J. S. Reaching through reading. *G/C/T,* 1978, *1* (5), 35.

Worcester, L. H., & Worcester, E. W. Things to consider when establishing gifted and talented programs. *G/C/T,* 1978, *1* (2), 29.

CURRICULUM MATERIALS

Creative prescriptions unlimited (Grades 1–2). Whittier CA: East Whittier City Elementary School District, 1974.

Creative prescriptions unlimited (Grades 3–4). Whittier CA: East Whittier City Elementary School District, 1975.

Creative prescriptions unlimited (Grades 5–6). Whittier CA: East Whittier City Elementary School District, 1976.

Creative prescriptions unlimited (Grades 7–8). Whittier CA: East Whittier City Elementary School District, 1975.

Eberle, R. *Scamper: Games for imagination development.* Buffalo NY: DOK Publishers, 1971.

Evans, J. *How to fill your toyshelves without emptying your pocketbook: 70 inexpensive things to do or make.* Reston VA: The Council for Exceptional Children, 1976.

Independent curriculum enrichment studies: Learning packages for gifted. Lafayette CA: Lafayette School District, 1976.

Karnes, M. B. *Creative art for learning* (curriculum for young children, 3 to 12 year level). Reston VA: The Council for Exceptional Children, 1979.

Karnes, M. B. *Helping young children develop language skills: A book of activities* (rev. ed.). Reston VA: The Council for Exceptional Children, 1973.

Karnes, M. B. *Learning language at home.* (Level 1, for children at 3 to 5 year level; includes four color coded groups of lessons that focus on four skill areas.) Reston VA: The Council for Exceptional Children, 1977.

Karnes, M. B. *Learning language at home.* (Level 2, for children at 6 to 9 year level; organized around four skill areas–manual, auditory, visual, verbal.) Reston VA: The Council for Exceptional Children, 1978.

Landis, M. *Class menagerie.* (A compilation of activities for secondary school students.) Lincoln: Nebraska State Department of Education.

Martin, B. A. *Social studies activities for the gifted student.* Buffalo: DOK Publishers, 1977.

Materials on creative arts for persons with handicapped conditions. Washington DC: American Alliance for Health, Physical Education, and Recreation, Information and Research Utilization Center in Physical Education and Recreation for the Handicapped.

Nazzaro, J. *Preparing for the IEP meeting: A workshop for parents.* (A 2 hour training package developed to help parents become productive participants in the IEP conference.) Reston VA: The Council for Exceptional Children, 1979.

Planning guide for gifted preschoolers: A curriculum developed with gifted handicapped children. Winston Salem NC: Kaplan Press, 1978.

Project SEARCH Curriculum Package (Arts and academics for gifted handicapped children.) Available from Educational Center for the Arts, 55 Audubon Street, New Haven CT 06511

SAVI, Science Activities for the Visually Impaired. Available from Lawrence Hall of Science, University of California, Berkeley CA 94720

Stafford, A. K., & Baxter, J. H. *Curriculum for an early childhood gifted and talented program.* Seneca SC: The Council for Exceptional Children (Bountyland School), 1978.

Teacher idea exchange: A potpourri of helpful hints. (A regular feature of the journal *Teaching Exceptional Children.*) Contact The Council for Exceptional Children, 1920 Association Dr., Reston, VA 22091.

IDENTIFICATION INSTRUMENTS AND MEASURES

The Abbreviated Binet for Disadvantaged (ABDA) by Catherine B. Bruch
Department of Educational Psychology
University of Georgia
Athens GA 30602

Baldwin Identification Matrix by Alexinia Baldwin
D.O.K. Publishers
71 Radcliffe Rd.
Buffalo NY 14240

BCP, Behavioral Characteristics Progression (Curriculum which can form the basis for assessing academic and adaptive behaviors of young children)
VORT Corporation
P.O. Box 11132
Palo Alto CA 94306

Biographical Inventory–Form U (1976)
Institute for Behavioral Research in Creativity
1570 South 1100 East
Salt Lake City UT 84105

BLAT, Blind Learning Aptitude Test
T. E. Newland
702 S. Race St.
Urbana IL 61801

California Achievement Tests
Del Monte Research Park
Monterey CA 93940

California Environmental Based Screen by Clifford Stallings
Western Social Research Institute
San Diego CA
Contact: Clifford Stallings

California Test of Mental Maturity (CTMM, 1963 Revision)
California Test Bureau
Division of McGraw-Hill Book Company
Del Monte Research Park
Monterey CA 93940

CIP—Comprehensive Identification Process
(screening test for 2½ to 5½ year old handicapped children)
Scholastic Testing Service
Bensenville IL

Goodenough-Harris Drawing Test (GHDT)
Harcourt, Brace & Jovanovich
757 3rd Ave., Test Department
New York NY 10017

Hiskey-Nebraska Test of Learning Aptitude (nonverbal)
Marshall S. Hiskey
5640 South Baldwin
Lincoln NB 68507

How Can Tests Be Unfair? (a workshop on nondiscriminatory testing)
    by Jean Nazzaro, 1975
The Council for Exceptional Children
1920 Association Drive
Reston VA 22091

IBAS—Instructional Based Appraisal System
(includes bank of sequenced objectives which can form basis
    for criterion referenced tests)

Edmark Associates
13241 Northrup Way
Bellevue WA 98005

IPAT Culture Fair Intelligence Tests (Scales I, II, and III)
  by R. B. and A. K. S. Cottel, 1963
Institute for Personality and Ability Testing
1602 Coronado Dr.
Champaign IL 61820

Learning Ability Profile (LAP)
Equ-a-Ex Corp.
First National Bank Building East
5301 Central NE, Suite 1520
Albuquerque NM 87108

Learning Accomplishment Profile (LAP) (assesses young children's
  adaptive and academic readiness skills)
Kaplan Press
600 Jonestown Rd.
Winston Salem NC 27103

Leiter International Performance Scale
C. H. Stoelting Company
1350 South Kostner Ave.
Chicago IL 60623

Leiter International Performance Scale
Special Education Materials, Inc.
484 South Broadway
Yonkers NY 10705

The Lorge-Thorndike Intelligence Tests, Multi-Level Edition
Houghton Mifflin Company
110 Tremont St.
Boston MA 02107

Metropolitan Achievement Tests
Harcourt, Brace, & Jovanovich
757 3rd Ave., Test Department
New York NY 10017

Minnesota Child Development Inventory (MCDI)
Behavior Science Systems, Inc.

Box 1108
Minneapolis MN 55440

Otis-Lennon Mental Ability Test
Harcourt, Brace, & Jovanovich
757 3rd Ave., Test Department
New York NY 10017

Peabody Picture Vocabulary Test (PPVT)
American Guidance Service, Inc.
Publishers Building
Circle Pines MN 55014

Project Improve by Joseph S. Renzulli (in *Report of the Task Force
    on Identification*, 1978)
Connecticut State Department of Education
Bureau of Pupil Personnel and Special Educational Services
Hartford CT

The Identification of the Gifted and Talented by Ruth Martinson
(rating scales and procedures to detect gifted culturally diverse children)
The Council for Exceptional Children
1920 Association Drive
Reston VA 22091

Ravens Progressive Matrices (nonverbal test of abstract reasoning
    using designs as test items)
The Psychological Corporation
394 East 45th St.
New York NY 10017

*Sample Instruments for the Evaluation of Programs
    for the Gifted and Talented* (1979)
TAG Evaluation Committee
Bureau of Education Research
Storrs CT

Slosson Intelligence Test (SIT)
Slosson Educational Publications
Dublin NH 03444

Standard Achievement Tests
Harcourt, Brace, & Jovanovich
757 3rd Ave., Test Department
New York NY 10017

Stanford-Binet Intelligence Scale (3rd Revision)
Houghton-Mifflin Company
110 Tremont St.
Boston MA 02107

Structure of Intellect (SOI) Test of Learning Abilities by Mary Meeker
SOI Institute
214 Main St.
El Segundo CA 90424
Contact: Mary Meeker

System of Multicultural Pluralistic Assessment (SOMPA)
Jane Mercer
Department of Sociology
University of California at Riverside
Riverside CA 92502

Torrance Tests of Creative Thinking
Scholastic Testing Service, Inc.
480 Meyer Rd.
Bensenville IL 60106

Wechsler Intelligence Scale for Children-Revised (WISC-R)
Psychological Corporation
304 East 45th St.
New York NY 10017

ORGANIZATIONS

American Foundation for the Blind
15 West 16th St.
New York NY 10011

American Printing House for the Blind
1839 Frankfort Ave.
Louisville KY 40206

American Speech and Hearing Association
9030 Old Georgetown Rd.
Bethesda MD 20014

Association for Children with Learning Disabilities
2200 Brownsville Rd.
Pittsburgh PA 15210

The Association for the Gifted (TAG)
1920 Association Dr.
Reston VA 22091

The Council for Exceptional Children
1920 Association Dr.
Reston VA 22091

National Society for Crippled Children and Adults
2023 West Ogden Ave.
Chicago IL 60612

PARENT/ADVOCATE GROUPS

Alabama

Alabama Association for Gifted and Talented
c/o Dr. Hiawatha B. Fountain
Birmingham Public Schools
P.O. Drawer 10007
Birmingham AL 35202

Arizona

Arizona Association for the Gifted and Talented
1745 W. Laurie Lane
Phoenix AZ 85021

California

California State Federation
Council for Exceptional Children
P.O. Box 2315
Pleasant Hill CA 94523

Gifted Children's Association of San Fernando Valley
17915 Ventura Blvd., #230
Encino CA 91316

Gifted Children's Resource Center
3923 Berryman Ave.
Los Angeles CA 90066

The Lyceum of the Monterey Peninsula
24945 Valley Way
Carmel CA 93921

MGM Program–Mentally Gifted Minors
Pasadena Unified School District
351 S. Hudson Ave.
Pasadena CA 91109

San Francisco Association for Gifted Children
P.O. Box 18233, Station M
San Francisco CA 94118

Connecticut

Teaching the Talented
University of Connecticut
Department of Educational Psychology

Iowa

Gifted and Talented Area Education Agency Communications Network

Area Education Agency 4
102 S. Main Ave.
Sioux Center IA 51250

Area Education Agency 6
9 Westwood Dr.
Marshalltown IA 50168

Area Education Agency 7
3712 Cedar Heights Dr.
Box 763
Cedar Falls IA 50613

Area Education Agency 12
1520 Morningside Ave.
Sioux City IA 51106

Area Education Agency 13
Halverson Center for Education
Box 1109, Route 1
Council Bluffs IA 51501

Area Education Agency 15
Box 498, Bldg. 40
Industrial Airport
Ottumwa IA 52501

Area Education Agency 16
305 Avenue F
Fort Madison IA 52627

Arrowhead Area Education Agency
P.O. Box 1399
Fort Dodge IA 50501

Grant Wood Area Education Agency
4401 Sixth St. Rd., S.W.
P.O. Box 1406
Cedar Rapids IA 52406

Green Valley Area Education Agency
Green Valley Rd.
Creston IA 50801

Heartland Area Education Agency
1932 S.W. Third St.
Ankeny IA 50021

Keystone Area Education Agency
Conlin Building
1473 Central Ave.
Dubuque IA 52001

Lakeland Area Education Agency
Cylinder IA 50528

Mississippi Bend Area Education
    Agency
2604 West Locust
Davenport IA 52804

Northern Trails Area Education
    Agency
P.O. Box M
Clear Lake IA 50428

Maryland

Allegheny County Association for Gifted and Talented Education
Frostburg MD

Maryland Coalition for Gifted and Talented Education
c/o Ms. Linda Barnett
5029 Nantucket Rd.
College Park MD 20740

Michigan

Macomb County Association for the Academically Talented
P.O. Box 266
Sterling Heights MI 48078

Michigan Association for the Academically Talented, Inc.
29976 Hennepin
Garden City MI

Oakland Association for the Gifted and Talented
P.O. Box 1011
Birmingham MI 48012

New Jersey

Gifted Child Society, Inc.
59 Glen Gray Rd.
Oakland NJ 07436

New Mexico

Albuquerque Association for Gifted and Talented Students (AAGTS)
Albuquerque NM

TAG (Division of the New Mexico Council for Exceptional Children)
University of New Mexico

New York

Advocacy for Gifted and Talented Education in New York State (AGATE)
State University of New York–Albany
1400 Washington Ave.
Albany NY 12222

Creative Education Foundation
1300 Elmwood Ave.
Chase Hall
Buffalo NY 14222

National Association for Gifted Children
76 Hall Ave.
New York NY 10956

National Association for Gifted Children
P.O. Box 267
Spring Valley NY 10977

New York State Association for the Gifted and Talented
P.O. Box 301
Valley Stream NY 11582

Society for Gifted and Talented Children
Box 589
Merrick NY 11566

Suffolk County Coordinating Council for the Education
   of Gifted and Talented
5 W. Second St.
Riverhead NY 11901

North Carolina

North Carolina Association for the Gifted and Talented
Department of Psychology
Meredith College
Raleigh NC 27611

Ohio

The Ohio Association for Gifted Children
c/o Joseph Virostko
1320 West 112th St.
Cleveland OH 44102

Pennsylvania

Pennsylvania Association for the Study and Education
   of the Mentally Gifted
Berks County PA

Tennessee

The Council for Exceptional Children
Tennessee Federation #242
Knoxville TN

Knoxville Chapter #98
Memphis Chapter #768

Texas

Richardson Association for Gifted and Talented, Inc.
439 Salem Dr.
Richardson TX 75080

Utah

Intermountain Center for Gifted Education
P.O. Box 7726
Salt Lake City UT 84107

Utah Parent Association for the Gifted and Talented
3448 Squirewood Circle
Salt Lake City UT 84120

Virginia

Advocacy for Gifted and Talented Education (AGATE)
17 Bradfield
Leesburg VA 22075

Fairfax County Association for the Gifted (FCAG)
P.O. Box 186
Merrifield VA 22116

Northern Virginia Council for Gifted/Talented Education
334 N. Washington St.
Falls Church VA 22046

Program for the Enrichment of the Gifted, Inc. (PEG)
P.O. Box 1687
Manassas VA 22110

Program for the Enrichment of the Gifted, Inc. (PEG)
4514 Kingsley Rd.
Woodbridge VA 22193

Signet
Prince William County–Gifted and Talented Program
Prince William County Schools
Manassas VA 22110

Washington

Northwest Gifted Child Association
P.O. Box 1226
Bellevue WA 98009

West Virginia

Kanawha County Association for Gifted Children
1617 Kirklee Rd.
Charleston WV 25314